THE MULTIFACETED LIBRARIAN

V.M. Mohanraj
Former Librarian

Ess Ess Publications

4837/24, Ansari Road, Darya Ganj,
New Delhi-110002
✆ : 23260807, 51563444
Fax : 011-51563334
E-mail: info@essessreference.com
url:http://www.essessreference.com

First Published **2006**

ISBN: 81-7000-479-9

Rs.400/-

Published by:
Ess Ess Publications
4837/24, Ansari Road, Darya Ganj, New Delhi-110 002
Tel: 011-23260807, 51563444 Fax: 011-51563334
E-mail: info@essessreference.com
url: www.essessreference.com

Printed in India at:
Printline, New Delhi

To
the memory of

SULU

the flame that had illumined my life for over half a century
and ever since has been ablaze in my heart
where it will keep burning
until the fire of life in me burns out

*

CONTENTS

PREFACE

Presumably, the title of the book reveals to some extent the point that I endeavour to focus on. It is, to put it tersely, the varied types of work that a librarian is expected to do. In fact, I have condensed into nine chapters a matter that would take actually nine volumes. In other words, the matter contained in each of the chapters, if elaborated, would take one volume of at least the size of this book.

I have pointed out in Chapter 1, 'Librarianship in India', that the modern librarian is an educator, facilitator, mentor, confidant, guide, resource person, social worker, appraiser and manager and that he is not merely a cataloguer, classifier and bibliographer as he had been till recent times. And with the computer entering the library, he has become an information disseminator too. In the subsequent chapters I have dealt with these different functions of a librarian.

Well, in the Chapter 'Facilitation', I have discussed in detail the technique of précis writing, which many librarians may think is quite redundant. But on several occasions, both as a college and a school librarian, I had to prepare brief summaries of magazine articles and even chapters from books for not only students but also educators. Besides, I thought practice in précis writing would help write abstracts, competence in which would enhance an accredited librarian's job opportunities. All abstracts are to be classified and indexed, which is the forte of a librarian and as such he will naturally be preferred, if he is good at abstracting, for editorial work in abstracting journals.

Eugene Garfield of the Institute of Scientific Information, USA, in a paper he wrote a few years ago, had prophesied that a hundred years from the end of the Second World War, the library would be an "Informatorium", considering the rapid rate at which science information had been increasing and the need for disseminating information for furthering scientific research. And now as he had foreseen the library all over the world is slowly but steadily becoming an "Informatorium". But the countries, like ours that have thrown off the yoke of colonialism after World War II have not been able to shake off the effect of hundreds of years of imperialist exploitation yet. As a result, a large majority of the people of these generally known as developing countries, is still steeped in abject indigence and resultant illiteracy. The library in these countries, therefore, is as much an instrument of social service aimed at spreading literacy and education as a centre for disseminating information. Anyway, whether it is an instrument of social service or an "informatorium" the librarian plays an important role as facilitator of education and research but in developing countries his educational activity takes him into the realm of social service.

Needless to say, a professional librarian should have a thorough knowledge of the techniques of classification and cataloguing – of course, information science too. In the chapter on classification the DC numbers given as examples are taken from the 16th edition of the DC Tables. I was wondering if I should write about the technique of preparing the card catalogue in the chapter, 'Cataloguing' because most libraries, including some non-governmental libraries are now automated and have either computerised or embarked upon a programme of computerising their catalogues. We are in the computer age now and no power on earth can reverse the trend or stop – why, even retard – the onward march of computerisation of libraries. In the not too distant future it can be expected, howsoever a pessimist one is, that most libraries in our country will be on the network of centrally computerised catalogues, with the result, card catalogues will soon be thrown into the dustbin of history. In the US all the libraries that I visited, had computerised not only the catalogues but the other areas of service as well. And I did not see card catalogues even in comparatively small county libraries. When I asked why there was no card catalogue, I was told that after the computer data base system had been introduced, card catalogues had been done away with altogether. That, in fact, prompted me to skip dealing with the technique of preparing card catalogue because hopefully, in our country too, it is bound to happen, sooner rather than later.

I have not gone very deep into the actual process of either classification or cataloguing; nor have I described the routine administrative duties of the librarian as a manager. All that is beyond the scope of this book, which as stated above is primarily to focalize not only the important role the librarian plays in all intellectual activities but also the different types of work that the librarian has to do in consequence.

Instead of dealing with the process and problems of resource selection in the chapter, 'Managerial Duties' of which it is the most important, I have devoted a separate chapter, 'Acquisition of Resources' for it. This is done precisely because it is the most important of the managerial duties of the librarian; if I club it with the other managerial duties, the reader will not realise the importance of resource selection.

I have given a list of a few selected Web Sites as Appendix 1 which, I believe, will be of help to librarians of all types of libraries.

V. M. Mohanraj

ACKNOWLEDGEMENT

I wish to express my gratitude to Bridget Chandramohan (*nee* Oswald), Headmistress, First Step School, Kozhikode, (formerly, Senior teacher at The Lawrence School, Sanawar and later HoD of the Economics Department at Frank Anthony Public School, Delhi) for her constructive suggestions which have been beneficially incorporated in the book. I am deeply indebted to Mondi Murugan, Librarian, The Lawrence School, Lovedale for the input of ideas based on his experience in library automation and to Dr. Prashant Mohanraj, Senior Scientist of the Indian Council of Agricultural Research for his input on abstracting journals. My thanks are due to T.P.Surendra, a veteran in the field of management, for going through the chapter on the managerial duties of the librarian, in the midst of his official work and offering critical suggestions. I am also thankful to Nisha Surendra who has read the whole of the first draft of the book with great care and has done a very helpful editing of the text, as a typical English teacher would do. I am grateful to Sandhya Vasantkumar, Librarian, Nilgiri Library, Ootacamund for promptly providing me with all the references that I wanted and occasionally taking the trouble of referring to the relevant books and passing on the information that I asked for, over the phone. I fully appreciate the unstinted co-operation extended to me by Daphne Sampson, Library Assistant and the entire staff of the Nilgiri library. I shall be guilty of gross impropriety if I do not thank Sumit Sethi of Ess Ess Publications, New Delhi, but for whom this book would not have seen the light of day.

1
Librarianship In India

Librarianship connotes 'the profession, authority and duties of a librarian' or in one word, 'the management' of a library, which is an institution that procures and keeps books, periodicals, and other printed and non-printed informational materials. All these are not kept for show or for future use but for using in the here and now by the members of the community that it is expected to serve and as such, it is basically a service institution. The modern librarian knows that it is not just a depository of documents and other informational material but a repository of information that has to be disseminated. The history of this institution is a long story, which commenced with the discovery of writing that marked the end of barbaric society and the dawn of civilisation. Since then, it had been growing and changing in harmony with the evolving human society, in the development and change of which it played an important role.

During the last century, particularly after the First World War, there has been an unprecedented expansion of the library movement in all developed countries. In India, the British colonialists had established a chain of libraries solely for the benefit of the British citizens in India. Later, however, when the newly emergent middle class began to assert itself the libraries established by the Colonial Power had to be thrown open to them. With the collapse of colonialism after the Second World War, the countries that attained independence, generally known today as developing countries, also witnessed the growth of this movement. Most developing countries had indigenous library movements in pre-colonial days but its growth was stunted when these countries were colonialised by the European powers. In our country, the British ruling class took a long time to appreciate our rich cultural heritage, in the meantime treating Indian learning with contempt, which had a crippling effect on our library movement.

So it is but a truism that the institution of library is not a new concept that the Indians learnt from the British, for, as we all know, there had been many manuscript libraries in the country – some of which world-renowned – since the 5th century AD. But, as pointed out above, there was a lull in the Indian library movement after the European imperialist powers set foot in India. Since then, the country had been ravaged by wars as a result of which the Kings and Nawabs who had been the patrons of learning had little time and funds to spare for libraries. Later, even when the country was under the colonial yoke, fired by the spirit of nationalism generated by the Freedom Movement, a modern library movement by the Indians had taken shape since the second decade of the 20th century, independent of the library movement initiated by the Colonial Power. And an organisation called the Indian Library Association with several branches that co-ordinated the movement came into existence. Consequently, many public libraries, catering to the needs of the Indians, sprung up in different parts of the country.

After the attainment of independence, with the spread of education and literacy and the resultant demand from the burgeoning literate section of the population as well as to meet the requirements of the fast growing industrial and commercial sectors there had been an unprecedented expansion of library movement in the country and consequently one by one several universities started training courses in librarianship. The movement got a tremendous boost with the passing of the Madras Public Libraries Act in 1948, the first one of it kind to be put on the statute book of any of the State governments in India. It was not, however, free from faults. Its greatest drawback was the appointment of the Director of Public Instruction as the *ex officio* Director of Public Libraries instead of a professional librarian as full-time Director to head the department. Nevertheless, the momentum that this law gave to the library movement resulted in the establishment of many adult and juvenile public libraries not only in the erstwhile Madras Presidency[1] but in all other parts of India as well and in less than a decade, by 1955, as statistics showed, 32,000 public libraries sprung up in the country. Although a good beginning, it was quite inadequate, considering the population of the country, which then stood at 360 million!

However, thanks to the above said enactment, like the ripples spreading in rings when a pebble is dropped into a well, the library movement spread in all directions. Thus, various types of libraries mushroomed, so to speak, all over the country. The mass education programme and the development of industries gave this Movement a further push. In consequence, several schools, all colleges and universities, research institutes and research and development wings of industrial units established libraries as their adjuncts to meet their specific requirements. And the already existing libraries of some of those institutions were strengthened and modernised. Except the few libraries established by the British for their officers and bequeathed, as it were, to this country when they left, no library in our country, of whichever category it is, functions as an independent unit. Those few non-governmental and independent institutions are run by Committees elected from among the members of those libraries and financed solely by the subscriptions paid by them. Consequently, those are exclusive libraries, not open to non-members and their development is retarded for want of sufficient funds. Among the other types of libraries, the public library, both adult and juvenile, is a government institution financed, staffed and controlled by the government to serve the community while the academic and specialised library is an auxiliary of an institution, an organisation or an industrial unit. As such, the library always serves the community or subserves the parent body of which it is an integral part.

As a result of the emergence of these diverse types of libraries, today, the librarian may be called upon to manage any of these categories of libraries, all of which, of course, are concerned with acquiring, organising and providing effective access to information. However, the function of the librarian, naturally, differs from category to category, in accordance with the requirements of the clientele of each of these types. As such, the librarian is a multifaceted professional person and is different from most other professional persons. The librarian, particularly the public librarian, has a great responsibility. His responsibility lies not just in maintaining the resource collection that has been entrusted to him for safe custody by the society. The public library being considered 'People's University', the librarian has to ensure that they are made use of not only by the educated class but also by the underprivileged of the community. This is undoubtedly a tall order that calls for a person committed to the cause of the oppressed and the welfare of the society in general.

The librarian, therefore, is not merely a manager but is much more than that. He is an educator, facilitator, appraiser, mentor, confidant, guide, social worker and manager besides being, as he ought to be, an expert in library techniques like classification, cataloguing, and preparation of bibliography to which has to be added Information Science, a new technique that has been introduced recently to enhance the efficacy of library service. He is an educator who has to instil the reading habit in children and may have to help students in their curricular and co-curricular activities. He is a facilitator of research and self-education. He is an appraiser as he has to estimate the worth from the point of view of its content in the case of printed and other materials and the utility value of all the resources, printed and electronic, before ordering them for the library. He may be constrained to act as mentor, confidant and guide to the youngsters who come into the library. He is a social worker who has to spread literacy and education among the illiterate masses and make sure, as stated above, that the youngsters and adults of both sexes who have been deprived of the opportunity to go to school make use of the resources in the library. He is also a manager who has managerial responsibilities, and an expert in library techniques, without which of course, he cannot be a librarian.

So it must be understood, the modern librarian is not what he had been in olden days when his duty was only to ensure the security and upkeep of the books that were in the library. He is, today, a professional person who makes it easy for the patrons to access recorded knowledge, both in printed and electronic media, and who disseminates information. Needless to say, without mastering the theory and practice of library techniques, he will not be able to arrange and keep the resources in a manner that will help the clientele of the various types of libraries, which have come up in the country since independence. No one can, therefore, be a librarian who has not undergone a general course in library and information science, which is the study of the principles and practices of library care and management and the application of computer to library services. He has to have a good grounding in library techniques like classification – a term, when referring to library technique means '*book* classification' – and cataloguing as well as information science, without which effective library service is not possible. Besides, as most libraries in India have books in the regional language as well as English, the librarian has to be good at those two languages. It would, however, be desirable if he has a good command of particularly English, which is the main library language. He need not be a polyglot but if his mother-tongue is not Hindi, it is better that he is also able, at least, to read and write *Devanagari* script. He will then be able to read the authors' names, titles and other particulars of books in Sanskrit, the classical language, and Hindi, one of the link languages of the country, to help him transcript when cataloguing, all the required particulars of books in those languages.

But all that is not enough. Those are only the basic requirements but with that alone, a graduate or post-graduate in library and information science will not be able to meet the demands of libraries of different types of institutions and organisations. In each type of library the kind of work that the librarian may have to do is different, for which he is not equipped. The university authorities concerned with the framing of the syllabus for the undergraduate and post-graduate courses are myopic and do not see beyond the confines of the Department of Library and Information Science or they are oblivious of the varied nature of the work in each type of library. In other words, they are yet to realise the need for specialisation in the field of librarianship. As a result, unlike in medical, engineering, law and various other professional courses, no opportunity is provided for the students of librarianship for specialisation.

It is imperative that no student of library and information science completes the course without specialising in the work of any one type of the library. They do not necessarily have to undergo a one-year or a two-year post-graduate course in the subject of specialisation as in the case of other professional courses. This can be done by making it compulsory at both the undergraduate and postgraduate levels for every student to offer one special subject as an elective and this could be related to any type of the library, the work in which the student desires to specialise. That is quite enough for the student to be able to carry out the work specific to that type of library. Similarly, 'Elements of Management' also must be an elective at the undergraduate level because in most libraries there will be only a library assistant and one professional librarian who *ipso fact* is the manager too. Or, as in big libraries the Chief Librarian under whom a few professional librarians, non-professional library assistants and other supporting staff may be working, will have to function as the general manager. If provision for offering an elective subject during the course of study cannot be made for any reason, universities should arrange to give in-service training to working librarians. The advantage of this is that the person can specialise in the type of library in which he secures a position on passing out of the university.

It may not be irrelevant here to point out that the Graduate School of Library and Information Science of the University of California in Los Angeles imparts specialised instruction in management for selected senior librarians. Similarly, in the UK the need for children's librarians to have special training for the work had been recognised by the Library Association long back. But this is imparted only to those who had experience and training in library work in general. In other words, it is a specialisation course. The Library Association holds an examination in 'Library Work with Young People', which was initially for a Specialist Certificate that could be taken by any student at any time. Later, it has been made an alternative part of the Final Examination and cannot be taken unless the candidate has passed the Registration Examination. This qualifies the candidate who has put in a minimum of three years' whole-time service in any approved library, for entry on the roll of Chartered Librarians, as an Associate of the Library Association. The syllabus comprises:

(i) Juvenile literature: This requires a detailed knowledge of modern children's books – reference books, books for various age-groups and for backward children. Besides, knowledge of the bibliographies and other guides to the field is also expected.

(ii) Child and adolescent psychology as well as their linguistic and reading ability at various ages.

(iii) Planning, equipment, organisation and development of children's library service.

(iv) A good knowledge of the educational system – its organisation, methods and objectives. The candidate should also know the book needs of the schools and school libraries and the possibilities for co-operation between schools and public libraries.

Apart from these, practical instruction is given in voice production and story telling. (McColvin, 1961).

The Indian society has to understand that all those engaged in any serious intellectual or educational activity cannot do without the help of the librarian, for he has to provide them with the necessary inputs, the resources for which are, to use a hackneyed expression, at his fingertips. Obviously, therefore, he plays the second fiddle and his hand works behind the scenes in any intellectual and educational activity that goes on in the society. Being an invisible hand, neither the person who seeks its help nor the society at large gives any credit to it and maybe because of that it always remains unappreciated and never gets the recognition that it deserves. For instance, a research project for which the librarian who has supplied considerable amount of information besides guiding the scholar to various other sources of information and bringing to his notice material for collateral reading is totally ignored. And the help he has rendered is not even acknowledged. But no librarian minds it because he is happy with what he has done, as all librarians usually would have developed service mindedness.

Of all the problems that beset the profession of librarianship in our country, the one that affects librarians materially and socially is that of salary and status as well as lack of promotional opportunities, which are, in fact, practically nil. The qualification and workload of the school librarian, for example, is no less, may be more, than that of the schoolteacher but in most private schools the scale of pay of the librarian is lower than that of the teacher. This also affects the status of the librarian. It may be recalled that as early as in 1953 the Secondary Education Commission constituted under the chairmanship of Dr. Lakshmanaswmi Mudaliar had recommended that the school librarian "should be on a par with other senior teachers in pay and status." (Lakshmanaswami Mudaliar, 1953). The Report has accumulated half a century of dust! In fact, even a quarter of a century before that, Dr. Radhakrishnan had called upon the public to respect librarians' "position as one not inferior to any other ...and recognise them as such, by securing for them adequate financial emoluments." (Radhakrishnan, 1929). This too had fallen on deaf ears.

However, in universities and in government colleges in most States, where the librarian is as much qualified as, and maybe more erudite than, professors, as far as the salary is concerned the librarian is on a par with professors but the society considers him inferior to a professor. The reason may be that librarianship is, so to speak, comparatively a new profession. Till very recently, anyone who could read and write was considered competent to hold the post of a librarian in a school, college or public library and that picture of a librarian still lingers in social memory. In short, the emoluments and the recognition that the librarian gets do not reflect the real value of the services that he renders to the intellectual world and society in general. It is because of the love of books or service mindedness – in most cases, both – that many a person continues in the profession that offers neither an attractive pay packet nor promotional opportunities.

In spite of such unattractive service conditions and adverse circumstances in which the librarian works, he does not fail to uphold certain principles. First and foremost he is conscious of the trust that the society has reposed in him and he always endeavours to live up to expectations. He is aware the he has been entrusted with the task of preserving and taking care of an invaluable treasure and no librarian is, rather can be, indifferent to the security of what is in his custody. He knows that the property that lies distributed in the shelves of the library cannot be evaluated in terms of the cost of the paper; the value lies in the ideas and facts that these tomes hold within them. It is the cumulative wisdom of the many bygone generations and that of the present generation. These are being collected and kept at one place for the benefit of the growing and yet to be born generations, for drawing on the knowledge gained so far they can take the society further on the road of progress.

The librarian, no doubt, is duty bound to respect the readers' intellectual freedom, not just because it is guaranteed under Art. 19 (1) (a) in Part III (Fundamental Rights) of our Constitution. He does it as a matter of principle. At the same time, he does not forget that he too has the right to the freedom of speech and the freedom to express any view. These freedoms, he should take full advantage of in the course of his social service to bring home to the illiterate and the marginalized, the root cause of their misery. And he should also make them realise that it lies within their power to change the conditions under which they exist currently. In one word, to use Freire's expression (Freire, 1977), he must "conscientise" them about the causes and remedies of their present plight and instil in them the necessary self-confidence to overcome it.

The librarian, therefore, has to realise that library service is primarily social service aimed at educational and cultural resurgence leading to the betterment of society and the empowerment of the downtrodden by conscientisation. This objective of the library commits him to the spread of literacy and education but single-handed, the librarian cannot undertake this stupendous task. So it presupposes the necessity to establish channels of communication with all organisations and institutions that are likely to have an interest in spreading literacy and education and enlist their co-operation, for this has to be done in collaboration with them if it has to succeed. This implies the need to liaison with the local social service organisations, political parties, trade unions, Women's organisations, educational institutions, Teachers' Unions, Students' Unions, international associations like the Rotary Club, Lions' Club and such other secular organisations. It is, therefore, imperative that the librarian is good at public relations.

Along with that, librarians will be able to serve the clientele and the community better, if the government adopt the 'Swiss-American System' as Lenin called it, in all the public libraries in our country. It may be of interest to recall in this connection, what Lenin had written in November 1917, immediately after the Russian Revolution, on the tasks of the Public Library in Petrograd. The situation in the erstwhile Soviet Union then and that of our country since independence, in the sphere of library service are strikingly analogous and the reason mentioned therein is applicable to our country if the word *tsarism* in Lenin's message is replaced by the word *colonialism*. He wrote, "Because tsarism had played havoc with public education over a period of many years, the library service in Petrograd is in a very bad state" (Lenin, 1917) and he suggested in the letter that the Swiss-American System must be introduced. He followed it up in June 1918 by summoning former State Council, State Duma and Book Chamber as well as all representatives of the libraries for a conference on centralisation of library organisation and introduction of Swiss-American system. In order to implement it, he wanted the following measures to be taken with immediate effect:

* "The public library – the former Imperial Library – must immediately start an *exchange* of books with *all* public libraries and state libraries in Petrograd and the provinces and with foreign libraries (in Finland, Sweden, *etc.*)
* The forwarding of books *from one library to another* must be made *post-free* by law.
* The library's reading-room must be open, as is the practice with *private* libraries and reading rooms for the *rich* in civilised countries, from 8.00 a.m. to 11.00 p.m. daily, *not* excluding Sundays and holidays.
* The required personnel must be immediately transferred to the Public Library from the various offices of the Ministry of Education...." (Lenin, *Ibid.*)

The Public Library in Petrograd corresponds to, for example, the National library in Kolata, the Connemara Library in Chennai or the Asiatic Library in Mumbai, which can have understanding with all the SAARC countries for exchange of books. Such an arrangement with neighbouring countries will mutually benefit and is as important as, if not more important than, trade agreements to foster good neighbourly relations. In fact, all libraries in our country, starting with each State, can arrange to have exchange of books among themselves. The additional personnel required if this system is to be introduced could be transferred from other offices but these would only be non-professional staff.

There is, however, no dearth of professional librarians, for today, universities in our country are producing a large number of librarians and they could be absorbed in our public libraries. Additional staff is necessary because no one can work continuously from 8 a.m. to 11 p.m., a duration of fifteen hours, at a stretch. It was realising this that Lenin had rightly asked for augmenting the staff of the Petrograd Public Library, without which, he knew that implementation of the reform, was not practicable.

In the context of our country, it may be pointed out that our libraries are in a bad shape because of our educational system, which was designed by the British to meet the requirements of colonialism, for which libraries had no part to play. Unfortunately, after the attainment of independence, the government had not been able to pay due attention to improvement of libraries in the country on account of the manifold problems affecting the security and integrity of the country that the government had been confronted with. The advantages that could be derived from what little improvement has been brought about are nullified by the attitude of the authorities. The authorities concerned have, an out-dated concept of library and library services; they do not view the library as a service institution and even access to the collection of books has been very much restricted. In fact, all those recommendations for revamping public library service in Petrograd can be implemented in our country without any difficulty whatsoever, but the initiative must come from the government under the control of which public libraries are. The most important of these recommendations is the introduction of *post-free inter-library loan system*, which can be easily introduced by a simple government order. The electronic revolution that has brought forth the computer as a tool for information retrieval has, today, opened up new vistas, making it easy to access as well as disseminate information. Hence, as several libraries of all types are already computerised or in the process of being computerised, we can even take a big leap forward to inter-linking of all the libraries in the country through Wide Area Network (WAN). We can begin with each city and in due course extend the facility to the district, the State and ultimately the entire nation. Such a network would not only facilitate the intellectuals, particularly writers and research scholars, to access the records available in any library in the country but also help self-education, recreational reading and even extension service.

Let alone inter-library loan system and inter-linking the libraries, our public libraries, even in this twenty-first century, do not allow the readers to borrow books other than novels. It is, therefore, imperative that first of all the authorities concerned with libraries are purged of their mediaeval mindset. Although we have introduced open access system in our public libraries, the authorities are more concerned with the security of books and keeping books in good condition than facilitating the use of books. So public libraries in our country are not permitted to lend out most of the informational books. As Ranganathan tellingly puts it, "the idea that it is accounting for every scrap of printed paper that is blown into the library and producing them for stock verification that forms library responsibility must go." (Ranganathan, 1950.) Most public librarians of today would naturally be in favour of lending out whatever books the readers want except, of course, encyclopaedias, dictionaries, gazetteers and such others, which are purely reference books.

It must be accepted that the worth of a library is not judged by the number of books or by the value and look of the books displayed in the shelves. In fact, a library, which has a huge collection of books, most of which are not soiled and look new, is not a library worth its name because the appearance of books betrays the fact that they are not being used. The criteria of a good library are not the size of the collection or the appearance of books but they are,

* easy access to the books in the library;
* the facilities provided for recreational, informational and investigative reading;
* the number of users; and
* the actual use being made of the books in the library.

The authorities justify themselves for imposing restrictions on the readers and for being wary of keeping the doors of the library wide open by pointing at the prevalence of vandalism and pilferage in libraries. This, however, is not a new phenomenon or one that is found only in our country; this is a problem that invariably every library in the world faces. As library membership burgeons, pilferage and vandalism of library resources would naturally increase. In other words, the more the number of members the library has, the greater this problem would be. Some libraries in Japan had found that the problem of vandalism and pilferage could be eliminated or at least considerably reduced if libraries install photocopying machines and take copies of whatever a member wants from a book – text or picture – at a nominal, if not free of, charge. Alternatively, either the member may be allowed to get it xeroxed at the nearest photocopying kiosk or the library can arrange to do this for the member at his expense. In addition, if funds permit, the library may provide every book with the necessary bar code and install the electronic warning system at the exit. Judging by the progress India is making in the field of electronics, it can be predicted that automation of libraries would be a reality in the not too distant future and all these may be within the reach of every library in the country.

As it is, if a member is caught indulging in this antisocial act, he may be warned that his membership would be cancelled in case this is repeated. And if he continues with such malpractice, the library is justified in asking him to make good the loss sustained by the damage, restricting his library facilities, suspending or revoking his membership. The appropriate action to be taken must be left to the discretion of the librarian who is the right person to judge, for only he would know, rather he is expected to know, the antecedents of the member. However, the librarian should not over-react; he must make sure that the punishment is commensurate with the enormity of the offence. But stringent rules are not desirable for libraries, whatever be the intention.

Anyway, what authority does the librarian have to impose a punishment like that? It has to be borne in mind that on principle no one, in this context no library member, can be penalised arbitrarily for any offence. But, then, what is it that constitutes an offence? An offence may be defined as the intentional commission of an act usually regarded as socially harmful and unambiguously specified as prohibited and punishable under the rules. So whatever action taken against a delinquent member, for example one that pilfers a book, has to be within the framework of certain rules and the purpose of making rules is only to prevent members causing *wanton* damages to or attempting to purloin library property.

But in judging and penalising a member who has either damaged or stolen a book, the principle of *mens rea* ought to be invoked in cases like the marginalised persons of both sexes, irrespective of their age. (Mohanraj, 2004 – for the connotation of the term 'marginalised') as well as those, both children and adults, who have a history of kleptomania. To put it differently, in those cases there has to be clear and unassailable proof of *mens rea*. On the contrary, the principle of *mens rea* ought not to come into play in penalising the physically and mentally normal persons – adults of all strata of society and children who belong to the privileged class. They have to be penalised, if they damage or are caught in the act of lifting or mutilating a book or cutting a page from a book or journal belonging to the library, irrespective of whether there is 'criminal intent' or not. Above all, the librarian should follow the spirit and not the letter, in enforcing the rules and should have the discretion to relax or even temporarily waive any rule in certain special cases.

Footnotes

1 The Madras Presidency comprised the entire Tamil-speaking area that is now Tamil Nadu, parts of the Malayalam-speaking, Telugu-speaking and Kannada-speaking areas barring the erstwhile so-called native States of Travancore / Cochin, Hyderabad and Mysore respectively.

2
The Interface

Library, as stated in the previous chapter, is an institution, which procures and keeps books, periodicals, and other printed and non-printed informational material for the use of the members of the community that it is expected to serve. Apropos of the etymology of the word 'library', it is said to be derived from the Latin word *librarium* meaning 'a chest of books', the root of which is *liber*, which means 'book' while the other word for the library, *bibliotheca*, is also borrowed from Latin. In Greek, the word used for 'library' is *bibliotheke*, which literally means 'bookcase' and is a combination of two words, *biblion* (book) + *theke* (receptacle), (World, 1981). Obviously, therefore, the original connotation of the word library was 'a collection of books,' which does not indicate the purpose for which the collection is made. However, it presupposes the necessity for a person to take care of it. That person who had been entrusted with the responsibility of maintaining the collection was designated 'librarian'. The librarian takes care of the collection and until about the Industrial Revolution, the collection of books and the librarian were maintained for the benefit of the intelligentsia or the educated few that constituted the privileged upper class of society and a large segment of society comprising the slaves and later serfs, who had been denied the right to education could not make use of the resources available there. As such, they had been cut off from the library altogether. However, today, as the library has become a resource centre, comprising not only books but also non-book informational materials, even the uneducated and the illiterate are expected to be drawn into the circle of library users.

Be that as it may, since its beginning, the library as a living institution has been a quadrifrontal complex, the four fronts or faces being

* the collection of books,
* the clientele,
* the community and
* the supplier

the librarian acting as the interface between the collection and the other three faces.

Of these four faces that constitute the institutional complex holding a collection of books, known as library, managed by a librarian (or librarians, the number depending upon the size of the collection as well as the number of users) for the benefit of the readers, the collection is the foundation of the complex. The librarian being the interface between the collection and the other three faces –the clientele, the community and the supplier – connects the collection and the reader. He also liaisons with the community, which is the fountainhead of present and prospective readers and the supplier, which is the conduit that brings in new materials to augment the collection.

The collection becomes a library only if there is a librarian to act as a liaison between the resources and the readers, for a collection that is not used by readers is not a library but a book dump or at best, a museum of books. Although in ancient times, the circle of readers was quite small and the librarian was primarily entrusted with the responsibility of ensuring security of the collection, he still did form the bridge connecting the collection and the clientele because readers could lay their hands on any item in the collection only through the librarian. As such, then and now, the librarian being the interface is, undoubtedly, the most important factor in the complex, in spite of the collection being the basis.

The relative importance of the first and the second faces has been changing over the years according to the importance each of these faces is given generally by the society of the given period. In short, depending on the changing societal needs that in turn changed man's attitudes, corresponding to the structural changes taking place in society, the importance gradually shifted from one face to the other. Suffice it to say, the factors that brought about changes in societal needs had chiefly been the economic condition of the people, the leisure available to them, the percentage of literacy, the burgeoning educated class, the production of books and other educational materials, printed and electronic, all of which had an influence on and were influenced by the library. A detailed discussion of this is beyond the scope of this book.

During the infancy of this institution, as stated above, the emphasis was on the collection and such an institution was maintained primarily for the preservation of the collection because there would not usually be more than one copy of each item. That this institution was called 'library', a word that is, as stated above, derived from a Latin word meaning 'chest of books' itself shows that the stress in those days had been on the 'collection'. It must be remembered that the collection, before the invention of printing, was manuscripts on palm leaf, birch bark and copper plates in India and in China they were on silk and bamboo while they were on clay tablets, papyrus, parchment and vellum in Egypt, West Asian countries and Greece. Naturally, therefore, the collection was more important at that time than the reader because it would have been impossible to replace if one item in the collection were to be lost or destroyed. To put it differently, the records kept in the library were basically meant to be preserved for conveying to future generations the knowledge acquired and accumulated till then and not for the enjoyment or enlightenment of the contemporaneous people; hence libraries were basically collection (book) centric. This was the case in the libraries of ancient Greece and riverine civilisations of Babylon and Egypt. The librarians of those libraries, as stated above, were concerned primarily with the proper upkeep and security of the documents that were under their custody in the library. The clientele was, so to speak, comparatively an insignificant face.

The libraries of mediaeval Europe and India, particularly those attached to Buddhist monasteries in India were used much more than those of the ancient world and so the reader was slowly gaining recognition as an important face. But the library continued to be record (book) centric, the reason being the same sociological factor, as in the days of the ancient civilisations. The primary concern of the librarian was still the collection in the library and the reader or the user was of secondary importance. But in due course, the situation changed. With the advent of the Industrial Revolution and the consummation of the objectives of the French Revolution and establishment of the First Republic during the 18th century, governments based on the principles of democracy began to sprout in Europe. The next century witnessed improved techniques of printing and production of books in large numbers. And by the turn of the 19th century when the impact of both these developments began to be felt fully on the European society the world of library was in ferment and a remarkable change came about in the concept of library. A library was no more just a repository of books intended for generations yet unborn; nor was it an institution exclusively for the use of the elite section of the society as it had been in the mediaeval period, for thanks to democracy, education spread to a wider section of society. The library became an institution that procured and kept books, periodicals, and other printed material for the use of the members of the community, irrespective of their socio-economic status.

Meanwhile, faced with the problems posed by the emergent educated class that had been growing at a rapid rate, librarians individually began to improvise techniques to meet the new situation and when the pressure increased they responded by putting their heads together to forge new standardised tools. As a result, classification systems and cataloguing codes that were universally applicable had been devised. These will be dealt with in detail in the relevant chapters. With the development of these library techniques, the librarian became a factor of utmost importance. The focus, now, was on the librarian. Unlike in olden days when libraries were managed by scholars or litterateurs, now persons who had been trained in the techniques of librarianship were required to manage libraries. In other words, not scholars or litterateurs but those with technical knowledge were preferred as librarians because the purpose of the library and the philosophy of service had undergone a drastic change. It was not any more for preserving the collection of records for the future but for the use of the present generation, the readers. None but a person trained in library techniques can assure that the readers get the benefit of the resources. So the library that had been book centric so far, became librarian centric – not that the importance of or concern for the security of books had diminished or the increasing importance of the readers and their right to use the collection not recognised. In fact, the recognition of the need for technically qualified librarian is the result of the growing importance of the readers. And the library is tending towards becoming reader centric. The librarian was now expected to help the clientele and to take necessary measures to widen the circle of readers and to maximise the use of the resources in the library. Of course, in those countries that had been colonialised by the industrialised nations of the West, this change occurred after the Second World War, with the collapse of colonialism all over the world. But in our country, thanks to an indigenous library movement, the importance of readers began to be recognised after the First World War.

The duty of the librarian does not now consist merely in ensuring the security of the collection or rendering minimal help to readers. The librarian is expected to use his technical knowledge of library management keeping in mind primarily the interest of the readers. But librarians had not been able to understand the real purpose of the newly developed techniques with the result they failed to adjust to this changing concept of librarianship. They continued to focus their attention more on techniques than on the clientele. This tendency among librarians to consider technical aspects as an end in themselves to the detriment of readers' interests made Dr. Radhakrishnan, in the late 1920s, to lament that "there is at the present day a temptation to overdo the mechanical part of a librarian's functions, such as card-indexing." And he adds, "the true functions of a librarian are of a much higher order. He has to guide the public taste and help the authors also." (Radhakrishnan, 1929). He was right, for the librarians of those early days of the development of library science, considered that their professional responsibility ended with classifying and indexing the books in the library and it took some more years for them to realise that technical work was just a means to an end. But again they stopped short of picking out the book(s) the reader asked for to be issued to him for reading at home or referring to in the library. In fact, the librarian was compelled to do this because the reader was not allowed to go into the stack room. Occasionally, however, if requested to, the librarian helped the reader find some information that he or she was seeking.

In due course, with the introduction of 'open access' system, this began to change slowly because now the reader himself could go to the shelves, browse on books and pick out the book(s) he wanted from the shelves. There is, therefore, no need for the librarian to do those chores and he is now free from the drudgery of going around and collecting the books applied for by members. He can, therefore, devote his time to help readers retrieve from the resources available in the library whatever information they are looking for. This is a much more challenging work and, of course, interesting too. Nevertheless, this service has been passive in the sense that the librarian is expected to act only when his services are solicited, until which time he sits at his table twirling his thumbs, if he is not having any technical or administrative duties.

Today, when the world is enmeshed in a network of communication channels, consequent upon the advent of the computer, the satellite communication system and what not, the reach of the librarian is not limited to the confines of the library; but extends far beyond the limits of the library and the boundaries of his country. It cannot be denied that with the revolutionary developments in the field of electronics coupled with the unprecedented explosion of information, the professional responsibility of the librarian as disseminator of information has increased manifold. And *ipso facto* the task of the librarian has become quite arduous. The librarian, therefore, collects the information regarding the latest findings of studies in any field that the readers are interested in, from the Internet and passes them on to the persons concerned. As such he does not wait for readers to come to him and seek his assistance; he goes around and asks readers if they would like him to help find the information they are looking for. A good librarian, therefore, does not sit at his desk with a grim, forbidding face but talks to readers, befriends them, and finds out their areas of interests. And he tries to get as much information on those topics, which are of interest to them, from various sources – printed and electronic – whenever he is not actively helping readers in the library. As such, today, the librarian is a resource person more than a technical person.

Consequent upon this, the days of book centric library are now *passé* forever. Similarly, the days when the librarian sat in his office behind his desk, his chair strategically placed to get a view of the exit door, or handed over the book or the journal that the reader asked for and left him to carry on his/her reading or research are also gone for good. In one word, the library has become *totally* reader centric. The readers' right to the resources is absolute and the librarian is the resource person. This has necessitated a change in the librarian's approach to the reader. He cannot afford to be impersonal as far as the reader is concerned. The librarian of today, thus, projects the human face of libraries. As a result, humanism is now a part of the larger code of ethics and the broad general principle of the modern librarian. What the adult reader expects in the library and of the librarian today, are a small patch of familiarity and a warm welcome and in addition to these friendly gestures, a sign from the librarian that contrasts with the detached coldness of the bureaucrat that characterised the librarian of yesteryears. A librarian whose mind has been imbued with modern concept and ethics of librarianship, therefore, realises that there is much more to the readers than their membership numbers and that his or her duty does not end with providing the readers with the book or the journal they ask for.

As for the juvenile readers, they look forward to a more bearable atmosphere that does not remind them of the rigid discipline, the formality and the matter-of-fact atmosphere of the classroom. The librarian shows himself as the friend of the young readers and respects their dignity; he regards them as human beings, empathising with their apprehensions, sharing their ambitions and acting as their mentor. No more does he look upon the youngsters as a potential nuisance; nor does he look at them as potential mischief-makers. And he does not also look down upon or talk down to a child. It implies bridging the generation gap and establishing a meaningful channel of communication with children, treating them as equals and appreciating each of them as a whole person and not merely as a reader. He accepts the fact that the juvenile, today, has as much right to library services as an adult has. As such, the ethics and principles of librarianship demands of the modern librarian, a holistic approach to readers – young and old, male and female.

Attention to individual details and cultural sensitivities is another important principle of librarianship today. In India, there are many areas populated with people of different customs, different religions and castes, different traditions and speaking different languages – in short, people of different culture. Apart from metropolitan cities, all towns and villages located in the border regions of every State have such multi-cultural, mixed communities. And such communities may comprise teachers, businessmen, engineers, doctors, lawyers, fishermen, mechanics and those engaged in various other vocations, not to speak of students, housewives and superannuated people. In all these places, inevitably, one linguistic, religious or professional group is bound to be in a majority. The librarian has to bear in mind that the public library is not the monopoly of the majority or any particular group of people; it is meant for all and its resources and services should reflect this pluralism of the local population. Books, periodicals and other materials being purchased for the library should cater to the interests and requirements of these diverse groups. The public librarian can succeed in popularising the library only if he recognises and respects this pluralistic demographic configuration of the community, which is bound to reflect in the constitution of its clientele. Correspondingly, although the resources of the libraries of schools and colleges of a given area have, first and foremost, to meet the requirements of the curricular and co-curricular activities of the institutions, these academic libraries cannot but take into consideration the social strata and the cultural group from which the students are drawn.

This new concept has brought about a revolutionary change in the librarian-reader relation. A modern librarian, therefore, adopts a reader centric philosophy, keeping the interests and needs of the reader in sharp focus, above everything else. Until recently when a reader came into the library for the first time ignorant of what treasure lay inside, he was left to discover it for himself; some succeeded and enriched themselves while some failed and left frustrated. But the librarian remained quite unconcerned and impassive. Not so, today! The librarian is concious of and recognises the fact that awe and diffidence are the most natural emotions of every new reader who enters the library for the first time. He, therefore, follows a customer care philosophy: the customer is a VIP and has to be attended to with due respect. As part of the customer care philosophy, the librarian should adopt the standard of customer care found in the business world, particularly the hospitality industry. In the context of the library, it is the member who is the VIP and as such no member, new or old, is left to fend for himself or herself. The moment a user enters the library, the entire system swings into action and personalised attention is given to each user making him feel at home.

If the user happens to be a youngster, on whose face fear and nervousness could, no doubt, be seen writ large, he is welcomed with a smile, after which the librarian has a chat with his parents when he assures them that the child would be taken care of. The child along with the parents may then be taken on a 'tour' of the library, the librarian or the assistant librarian acting as a 'tourist guide' to acquaint the youngster with the library. It is necessary to take the parents along so that they too come to know of the invaluable treasure that lies spread out on the shelves of the library and the services that the library renders. Possibly, this introduction may help draw the parents too into the fold of the clientele. In fact, every member of the staff who comes in contact with the young reader gets involved in this process of initiation The best way to allay the fear of a novice and give him confidence is not only by avoiding a 'Big Brother' attitude and by treating him as an equal but also by communicating with him in a language that he comprehends. So when explaining to him the layout and showing him the books and various instructional materials as well as the catalogue of the library, simple language, devoid of any technical terms that would confuse and alienate him, has to be used. Of course, it is imperative that the librarian gets in touch with the parents of all juvenile users and invites them to the film shows, puppet shows and such other special programmes arranged for the juvenile members of children's library and adult library that has a children's section. We shall not discuss here 'Library Festivals', which shall be dealt with in Chapter 5, 'Extension Service'. Incidentally, it is desirable that children's library and children's section of an adult library is managed by a female librarian, for a woman makes a better children's librarian than a man. (Mohanraj, 2004.)

And to ensure that there is no flaw in the implementation of this reader centric policy, a 'Library Service Feedback Book' (which is different from the Suggestion Book, usually kept in libraries for readers to suggest the books they would like the library to procure) is kept in the reading room of the library for getting readers' feedback on the services being rendered by the library. And the readers must be encouraged to write candidly whatever they feel about the library services. Of course, it will be of no use if the librarian does not go through it before the periodical meeting of the library staff and discuss at the meeting the suggestions given by the readers to improve those aspects of library service that the readers have adversely commented upon. And, if practicable, those must be implemented. Otherwise, the librarian must discuss with the reader concerned after thanking him/her for the interest being shown in the library and explain why the suggestion, though valuable, cannot be put into practice. All these go a long way in making reader centric library, reader friendly.

No doubt, three of the Five Laws of Library Science enunciated by Ranganathan – "Every reader his book; Every book its reader; and Save the time of the reader." – do, to some extent, help make the library reader friendly (Ranganathan, 1951). He theorises that by improving library tools and techniques to

(i) make it easy for readers to lay their hands on the books they want;

(ii) bring to the notice of each reader the book he or she may be interested in; and

(iii) enable the reader to get whatever he/she wants in the shortest time possible,

would help make the library reader friendly. Modern philosophy of library service, on the other hand, lays emphasis on the human factor, rather than on the machinery, by focusing on librarian-reader relation for making the library reader friendly. This does not mean that library tools and techniques are unimportant or to be ignored. In fact, they too should reflect the human face of the library. However, it must be borne in mind, the library staff is primarily what makes the library reader friendly or otherwise. However much library tools and techniques are improved, no library would be reader friendly unless the librarian and his team are. Of course, the attitude of the team comprising professional assistants, clerical assistants, technical assistants like, for example, computer experts and the attendants depends on that of the Chief Librarian. Hence, both the library staff and library techniques have to be reader friendly, in which case alone the three laws would effectively come into play and enable readers to take advantage of library resources to the maximum.

But this is made possible only if the rules of the library are also reader friendly and this lies with the authorities concerned, for it is they who frame the rules, not the librarian. In the case of public libraries and libraries of government schools and colleges, the authority is either the Local Self-government, the State government concerned or the Central government, while in the case of universities and private schools, it is the Syndicate, the governing body or the Management of the institution concerned. In the libraries of ancient times the rules barred the entry of a vast majority of the people and even the few who had access were not permitted to use the records as freely as it is now after the introduction of the open access system. The library, then, was more a depository of records than a library in the modern sense of the term and the librarian guarded them like the legendary serpent guarding the treasure. The rules were to some extent less restrictive in the mediaeval period, although books could be referred to within the precincts of the library by an exclusive clientele. The modern period, which as far as the library movement is concerned, commenced with the advent of the Industrial Revolution, witnessed a change in the attitude of the library authorities. Liberalism and principles of democracy that characterised the society in general began to be reflected in the library, too.

Consequently, the doors of the library have been thrown open to the people at large although the majority is not able to take advantage of this facility, even today. The reason for this inability of a large number of people and the steps that the library should take to enable them to make use of the library shall be discussed in Chapter 5, 'Extension Service'.

Although the library works on the principle that the books therein are meant to be used it must be made clear that not all the books that are in the library can be allowed to be borrowed or taken for reference without restriction. The library has two sections – the reference section and the lending section. The former contains books meant for reference only and not to be taken out of the premises under any circumstance while the other, the latter, has books that can be borrowed and can be taken out for reading at home. The books in the reference section are usually encyclopaedias, dictionaries, gazetteers, atlases, over-sized and under-sized books, rare and out-of-print books, very expensive books and serials like Yearbooks and such other publications. Of these, over-sized and under-sized books, rare and out-of-print ones and very expensive publications are, in most libraries, kept in closed bookcases and are given out for reference, only if requested for. The other reference books are kept in open shelves and all the rest of the books would be in the lending section. Occasionally, certain book(s) in the lending section, if the librarian deems it necessary, may be declared "For Reference Only" and transferred to the reference section or may be lent for shorter periods as may be necessary.

This is not done arbitrarily. The library, like any institution, is governed by certain rules. Although the library is open to all those constituting the community that the library serves and the members have the right to use the entire resources of the library, these as well as various other matters concerning the services rendered by the library are regulated by rules. The factors that necessitated libraries also to have a set of rules and how these are to be enforced have been dealt with in the previous chapter. Here we shall discuss what kind of rules the library should have.

It is, of course, unfortunate that there are, even among the educated class, antisocial elements who mutilate or filch books and periodicals, for paradoxically education, even university education, does not make a person cultured; nor does it instil social consciousness. So among the members of a library, though all of whom are usually drawn from the educated class, there will be a few biblioklepts - not considering kleptomaniacs - and vandals. That such persons are also found among those who occupy very high official positions and those of the affluent class - in short, all those whom we normally do not expect to stoop to indulge in such anti-social acts - cannot be denied. The percentage of such undesirable elements would, however, be very small, maybe hardly .001 percent of the total number of members. So rules of the library should not be framed, presuming that everyone who steps into the library is prone to such antisocial behaviour but on the assumption that all persons are honest, unless proved to be otherwise. In fact, one of the reasons for vandalism or pilferage is that the rules are too strict and are applied too rigidly.

So the rules are to be framed basically to make it convenient for the readers to use the library freely. No doubt, rules of all libraries, though apparently restrictive, in effect enhance the freedom of the users, who, unfortunately, think otherwise. The librarian may, when situations arise, explain to them how the rules help rather than hinder the use of the library. If a member talks in the library, he must be reminded of the rule forbidding members from conversing loudly in the library and told that the rule is only to help everyone work undisturbed in the library. And he may be asked how he would feel if someone else talks loudly when he does some serious reading. Similarly, the rule that restricts the number of days that a member is allowed to keep a book borrowed from the library, may seem to be curbing the freedom of the reader but it actually prevents one member monopolising a book thus infringing upon the right of other members to read that book. Again, the rule that "any book, which is temporarily in special demand may be lent for shorter periods or may be temporarily declared a reference book" may be thought of as irksome but that too is helpful to the members like the one just mentioned above. Keeping certain books like encyclopaedias, dictionaries, gazetteers, yearbooks and such other works strictly for reference also is to ensure that members get those books to refer to whenever they want and carry on research or self-education without any hindrance.

In keeping with the spirit of democracy, the rules should enhance the freedom of the users and should not be inhibitory. In other words, the set of rules must be conducive to *facilitating* and should *not be a deterrent* to, the use of the books and the library; it should not be such that the members regard it as a barrier between them and the resources. If it is such that the members consider it a code that enhances their freedom to use the library and the resources therein, it would help increase not only the use of the library but also the circle of members. Most importantly, the rules should be brief and in a simple, straightforward language avoiding legal style and expressions but legally tenable.

3
Facilitation

The people of ancient India looked upon the owner of a library as a learned man – and that, indubitably, he would be – because he would have read critically, evaluated and be thorough with the literary works that had been in his collection. And to this concept of an owner of a private library may be attributed the origin of the old Sanskrit aphorism, *kosavaan aachaaryaha.* In ancient India there were no books of the kind that we have today; but only manuscripts on palm leaves or birch bark, called *granthas* in Sanskrit; hence the word *kosavaan* means 'one who possesses granthaas'. The above-mentioned adage may, therefore, be taken to mean, 'the possessor of a collection of *granthaas* is a preceptor'. A collection of *granthaas* was, then, the library. So the Sanskrit saying can be translated as 'the possessor of a library is a preceptor', which implied scholarship and in those days a scholar alone was recognised as an educator. And rightly so because a teacher, then, was invariably erudite.

Obviously, therefore, having a library of one's own did indicate owner's scholarship in days of yore in our country. The practice of collecting manuscripts merely as a hobby, was not known, then – 'bibliophily' (if collection of manuscripts could be called so because the combining form *biblio* means 'book' or 'books') probably, started with the rise of monarchical States. The kings and nawabs in the India of those times, some of whom were illiterate, collected manuscripts, perhaps, merely to satisfy their ego. Akbar, the Mughal Emperor, for instance, who it is generally believed was illiterate – he was an ardent lover of learning though – is reputed to have a private collection of manuscripts, to equal which, there was none in India or in any country in the world at that time. It cannot be denied that most kings in India admired scholarship and enjoyed the company of scholars. But it is not known if any of those kings themselves were scholars; a few of them, no doubt, were litterateurs. Harsha, for example, is said to have written three plays, although it cannot be said with certitude that he himself wrote them; possibly they were written by his ghost writer(s). Bahadur Shah II, the last of the Mughals, however, was a poet of which there is no doubt, for he is known to have composed poems even when he was incarcerated in the Red Fort. Anyway, many of the kings in India had excellent libraries in their palaces, the librarians of which were usually scholars or litterateurs like, for example, Krishna Bhatta, a poet and Amir Khusrav, who was also a poet.

The Sanskrit saw, *kosavaan aachaaryaha,* however, does not connote that in those days whoever had a library of his own was necessarily engaged in teaching; it only indicates that he was a learned man as he would have read and assimilated, as it were, all the manuscripts that were in his possession. This is in a way true of the modern librarian also. There is no gainsaying the fact that, today, the librarian of any type of library, though not the owner of the collection of resources over which he presides, is virtually in possession of the library. And he is expected to know every book – a good librarian, no doubt, does make it a point to acquaint himself with all the books in the collection – that is on the shelves. He would not have read them all. Of course, today, when the market is inundated with books and periodicals it is impossible for even the most voracious reader to read all the books. As any library, these days, even the one in a remote village, may have thousands of books on various subjects, no librarian can find the time to read all of them. But he would, certainly, have skimmed through all the books and at least glanced through the periodicals in the library to make himself familiar with their contents. Indubitably, therefore, the librarian is sure to have a general idea of the content of each of the books that the library has and the periodicals that the library subscribes to. Even in huge libraries like for example, the National Library, Kolkata, the librarians working there, would be knowing vaguely at least, all the books that are on the shelves. This is imperative if they have to fulfil their responsibility as teachers, for the librarian, today, is primarily a teacher. But all modern librarians are, certainly, not scholars although there could be a few who are. The difference between the modern librarian and the owner of a library of ancient times is thus purely technical.

The modern librarian, as stated above, is an educator in the sense that he helps the process of education but to call him an educator is to reduce him to a mere teacher, ignoring the larger role he plays in the field of education and research. Hence, to be precise, as Thomas Kuhn conceives in the context of today, when there is, as he says, a paradigm shift in educational practice in schools, the emphasis being laid more on learning than on teaching, a teacher is a facilitator rather than an educator. How far this is true of the teacher in the context of India today, is a million-dollar question but that is beside the point. However, in the case of the Indian librarian, what Kuhn says is quite true because the librarian has always been a facilitator, although of late many a school librarian has to actually teach the children library techniques to enable them to use the library and books. Anyway, it is appropriate to regard the librarian, whether of the academic, public or special library, as a facilitator because the library is an institution where the users are facilitated to learn on their own.

What is facilitation or what is the duty of a facilitator? Facilitation, in the context of a library, may in simple terms be defined as service to readers. Generally speaking, a facilitator is a person who assists another – a person who makes it easy for another person to do a work. In other words, a facilitator lessens the work of another person, thereby making it easy for him to carry out the task he has on hand. That exactly is what the librarian does – he facilitates the work of educational and intellectual workers, like teachers both at the school and university levels, research scholars, journalists and authors as well as those involved in self-education. He also facilitates students to learn on their own and above all, he is a facilitator to the illiterate too.

In fact, even the Chief Librarian of any type of library, although the management of the library is his primary duty, is much more a facilitator than a manager. Today, the clientele being the most important of the four faces of the library, which is an informal educational institution, the primary duty of the librarian is to attend to the educational and intellectual needs of the reader. Hence basically, his duty is, like a teacher, facilitation of learning. Any librarian, irrespective of the type of library he is in charge of or whatever be the technical work he does in a large library with more than one librarian, cannot absolve himself of this responsibility. He is an educator in the sense that in the public library he facilitates literacy drive and self-education, in the academic library, he educates by facilitating the people concerned to learn and to teach, the two aspects of the process of education. In special libraries, like, for example, those of research laboratories, publishing houses of periodicals, parliament/legislative assemblies and law courts he facilitates the intellectual work being carried out at the respective parent institutions. All the technical work that the librarian does, in the final analysis, is intended to facilitate facilitation.

Let us now go into the work of the librarian as a facilitator in each type of the library, briefly. There are, as you know, many types of libraries – the adult public library, the children's public library, the school library, the college library, the university library and the special library. In each of these types, the facilitation work differs. In other words, the type of library determines the kind of facilitation work that the librarian has to do.

In an adult public library, the librarian facilitates the process of learning in the case of the illiterate and those who are interested in self-education and he may have to facilitate the process of investigation in the case of scholars involved in research. In the process of spreading literacy and education among the under-privileged, he puts on the mantle of a teacher in the traditional sense of the term, for he literally teaches the illiterate children and adults. More of this aspect of a public librarian's work, which he carries out as a social service shall be dealt with in detail in the chapter, 'Extension Service'; hence a discussion of it would be superfluous here.

The public librarian, as stated above, facilitates self-education also. Many a library user may be interested in improving his educational qualification either to get a better job than the one he/she is already holding or to secure a promotion therein, for which the hopeful incumbent may require a higher qualification. So he or she comes to the public library, which usually may have *Regulations and Syllabus* of various universities in the country. In addition, the library may also have previous years' question papers or at least model questions, of the universities in the State in which the library is. Apart from that, the library is sure to have books that would help him prepare for the examination, which he is planning to take and he may even find the prescribed textbooks of the universities in the State. Public libraries in metropolitan cities and most big towns in our country are quite well-equipped as far as printed resources are concerned and it is not rare to see many aspirants to the Indian Administrative Service and Banking service for example, coming to the public library to prepare for the respective competitive examinations. Similarly, research scholars also come to these public libraries to collect materials for or refer to some books in connection with the projects they are working on or even for collateral reading material. And in all these cases, a well-read public librarian successfully acts as facilitator.

The children's public librarian too facilitates self-education. She – children's librarian should preferably be a woman – guides the young members' reading besides leading them on to books of higher and higher standard with a view to better their reading tastes. This too is, obviously, an educational work that can be classed as facilitation. A committed children's librarian conducts story-telling sessions, play reading and such other activities that help create in the youngsters a love of books. Besides, she usually collaborates with the librarian of the adult public library in the work of spreading literacy and education. And if she is working in the children's section of an adult public library she may have to help out her colleague(s) in the adult section many a time in carrying out the work of facilitation of adult users.

In the school library, facilitation includes various kinds of work, for the librarian has to facilitate the process of not only learning but teaching as well. Although he facilitates learning as much as a teacher does, he is not a teacher in the usually understood sense of the term, for he does not teach according to a set timetable as a teacher does in the classroom. And he is not constrained by curriculum and syllabus or the pattern of examination as a regular teacher is. So in the school library, educands and educatees are not taught but are facilitated to learn on their own. A good school librarian relates the library to the classroom, when naturally the children come to the library to work on their assignments. And the librarian has to guide them to find the information they need in connection with their assignments. Similarly, teachers may give the children projects for which too the children, while researching for it, would seek the help of the librarian. And the librarian, in the course of helping them will teach them the use of books and library. This involves teaching them how to find the information they want from the book with the help of the table of contents and index and in addition, he may have to train them to take down notes from source books. Besides, he will be acquainting them with the classification system and the use of catalogue as well as the layout of the shelves, without an elementary knowledge of which the children would get lost in the library. Of course, at the primary level, the librarian has to teach them the ethics of library – what to do and what not to do in a library. And he has to initiate every child into the world of books and also create in him a love of books, which involves story-telling sessions and various other activities. The educational aim of all this is to instil the reading habit in children. Often, he will have to facilitate the process of teaching by collecting any information that teachers of various subjects may be asking for in connection with the lessons they are taking.

The college or the university librarian may not have as much facilitation work as the school librarian has. Adolescents that the students are and having a bloated sense of self-importance as college students, many of them may initially resent if the librarian in good faith offers to help them. So for a few weeks or months, they should be left to themselves. Soon, however, they would realise the need for the librarian's help. However, the librarian would not have to teach the students how to use books and library. A majority of the students would have come from schools that have no library worth the name but even they will pick up by themselves the system of classification, the way the books are arranged in the shelves and the intricacies of the catalogue. Anyway, in the college library the librarian's facilitation work is limited to guiding the students and the staff find the source books containing the information they are seeking. Of course, research students (not many colleges have research students on the rolls but invariably all universities have) would often approach the librarian for help. However, professors may frequently request the librarian to pick out a few books dealing with topics that they are planning to teach the next day or week. In such cases, the librarian collects the books and flags them so that the professor concerned need not waste time to find the pages in the books dealing with the topic. And the librarian may have to prepare summaries of articles in periodicals or a chapter in a book for students and professors. Besides the librarian should not fail to bring to the notice of the professor concerned articles in journals that may be of interest to him.

However, librarians of special libraries – library of a research institute like for example the Indian Historical Research Institute, research institutes of the Council of Scientific and Industrial Research, Indian Council of Agricultural Research and such other organisations, besides libraries of the R & D sections of industrial units like that of the Tata's for instance and of those like the South Indian Textile Research Association and the Defence Research and Development Organisation, those of the parliament and legislative assemblies, Bar Council and Court libraries, and such others – may have the work of facilitation much more than librarians of any other type of library, including the university library. The assistance given to the clientele in a special library is quantitatively more and qualitatively different from the services rendered to the clientele of any other type of library.

It is true that the man-power required to manage a library is determined by the collection it holds, the size of the clientele, the number of books issued per day, and the nature of the service expected, each of which indicates the use being made of the library by its clientele. You may have to take into consideration all or any set of these factors in deciding on the size of the personnel required to manage it. All the factors mentioned above except one, however, would be totally misleading and cannot be relied upon as criteria for fixing the strength of the staff in a special library. Unlike a public library and academic libraries for example, a special library seldom purchases books of imaginative literature like poetry and fiction and rarely, if at all, even popular books of informative literature but only highly technical and erudite works pertaining to the discipline(s), with which the parent institution is concerned. And so the library may not have on its shelves as many books as in a public library or university library, the shelves of both of which would be overflowing with books of imaginative literature and popular as well as scholarly works on various disciplines. The daily issues also are bound to be much less than and the number of users too, needless to say, would be much less than those in any other type of library. The one exception is the nature of service. But those who have the authority to decide on the number of professional and non-professional staff needed in the special library are totally ignorant of the nature of service in a special library. And they are ignorant of their ignorance as a result of which they do not consult the librarian about the personnel required.

Consequently, most special libraries are, it has been found, usually under-staffed having only one professional librarian who, naturally, finds it difficult – rather, practically impossible – to carry out the technical and administrative work of the library as well as facilitation work. As stated above, the criteria followed in deciding on the personnel of other academic libraries like school and college libraries do not hold good in the case of special libraries. In public and university libraries many professional librarians are appointed based on the size of collections and the clientele as well as the heavy circulation. The authorities concerned do not realise that the service to be rendered by the librarian of a special library is much more onerous than it is in any other type of library, including university and public libraries. It is not possible for one librarian to cope with the work in a special library. It cannot be overemphasised that facilitation, cataloguing and to some extent even classification of books in a special library are all quite difficult tasks. Although, there may not be many additions in a year, the cost of technical books being usually quite high and the outlay for books limited, classification and cataloguing of these books may take considerable time. Classifying technical books needs to be given a lot of thought and in several cases, the librarian may have to consult subject experts and this involves time. Equally, if not more, time-consuming is the work of cataloguing. With the advent of computers no cumbersome clerical work that takes a lot of time is involved in cataloguing, but many books of informative literature may have to be provided with several analytical entries for subjects. This has to be given considerable thought to and it naturally takes a good deal of the cataloguers time. Even if the catalogue is computerised, the librarian of the library of each unit has to provide the input for subject analytics (until centralised cataloguing system is adequately developed in India). Subject analytics are also to be made for parts of a book when all the subjects that the book deals with are not covered by the subject heading for the main part of the book

It is, particularly, in the libraries of research institutes and industrial units that have Research and Development wings the work of the librarian as a facilitator takes much of his time. All such institutions are always engaged in various research projects and the library attached to any such institution may, undoubtedly, be subscribing to many learned journals pertaining to the discipline(s) with which the parent institution is concerned. The librarian has to keep himself informed of the projects on which the research scholars are working and go through all the journals to see if articles or papers connected with any of the projects under way appear in them. Similarly, there would be, occasionally, if not usually, several articles of general nature, which though not directly connected with any of the projects that they are working on, could be of use to the researchers. Usually, many of the scholars would not take the trouble of perusing them. But the librarian has to and if he thinks that they have some bearing on the project that a scholar is working on, he should not fail to bring all these to the notice of the research scholar concerned. Even daily newspapers may carry news reports or articles relevant to the projects being carried out in the parent institute. A good librarian will take clippings of such materials, index and file them after circulating them among the scholars concerned for information.

These alone are not enough. Many a time, the librarian may have to prepare – a good librarian does prepare – brief summaries or abstracts of such articles and circulate them among research personnel. All learned journals, of course, invariably carry abstracts of papers appearing in them. These abstracts must be copied, indexed and duly filed. But apart from these journals, the library may be getting monographs, reports of proceedings of conferences, as well as copies of unpublished doctoral theses and various such documents besides subscribing to several or a few periodicals of general nature. Preparation of abstracts or even précis of all such documents and materials (however unimportant they may seem to be then, they might be of use at some point of time in the future) indexing and filing them falls within the purview of the duties of the librarian of a special library.

It is, therefore, desirable that those who take up the profession of librarianship know the technique of writing précis as well as abstract. These two are, no doubt, very different but if one knows to write a précis, it is not difficult to write an abstract. The librarian does not have to know the subject of the passage of which he is going to write the précis but in order to write an abstract of a research paper, particularly scientific paper published in a learned journal, he should have sufficient knowledge of the wider subject that encompasses the topic under discussion. For example, it is difficult to write an abstract of a research paper on a topic related to quantum physics or nuclear technology, without a good background in physics. At the same time, it is essential, as pointed out in the chapter, 'Librarianship in India', that the librarian has a good command of the English language, for otherwise it may not be possible for him to carry out this task. He should be able to comprehend fully what he reads and express precisely the idea(s) that he wants to convey.

Let us now see what a précis is and how to write a précis. Borrowed from the French, the word *précis* is derived from the Latin, *praecisus* meaning 'abridged' or 'cut off' and is used in English to mean 'summary,' 'abstract,' or 'a concise or abridged version of an article or a passage'. But there is a difference between a précis and an abstract as well as an abridgement, a summary or a paraphrase. It is true that an abridgement like précis is a condensation of the original; so is a summary as well as a paraphrase. But a précis is not to exceed a third of the number of words of the original text whereas there is no such restriction in the case of an abridgement, summary or paraphrase.

We are concerned with précis writing and abstracting only. It must be borne in mind that both these are not easy as it may seem; they call for concentration, cogent thinking and the ability to grasp the essence of the passage of which a précis or an abstract is to be written. First of all, the précis/ abstract writer is expected to dive deep into the passage or piece and find out the kernel, which he has to extract, for which he should read the piece carefully. He may have to read the passage more than once – maybe, several times in certain cases – to comprehend the main idea that the author of the piece or article wants to convey. In other words, the librarian should not fight shy of reading it as many times as he needs to understand the full import of the passage and if necessary, mark the phrases and words the meanings of which he is not sure of and consult the dictionary, after which he must read the passage again.

The précis has to be given a short, crisp title that would bring out the subject. The key sentence, which may be either at the beginning or at the end of the passage, will help you decide on the title. Now you can confidently proceed to the next step, which is the first step for writing the précis/abstract and that is to note down the points. Again read through the passage and select the important points/keywords and note them down. The points constitute the skeleton around which the précis is to be moulded; hence the points should vividly present before you the core or the main theme of the original passage. Before commencing to write the précis, remember that you have to condense the passage to one third of its length. It is, therefore, imperative that you count the number of words in the original passage in order to make sure of the number of words permitted so that you don't exceed it. You are now ready to make out the first draft.

The précis should be in your own words, shorn of all flowery expressions, figures of speech, repetitions, and unwanted details. In other words, it has to be written in simple, direct, grammatical and idiomatic English, taking care not to use colloquialism, clichés and archaic expressions. Whatever is in direct speech in the original must be put in indirect speech. The précis writer need not follow the sequence of the original passage but should not miss any point; the meaning/purpot has to be clear. And the précis should express exactly what the author has stated, without any comments and adding any facts. In case any factual mistakes are found in the original the précis writer is not expected to correct them or point them out; his presentation must strictly adhere to the original, for the précis writer is not an editor. This does not, of course, mean that even printing errors of spellings of words are to be repeated as such.

Once you complete the draft, check the length of the précis and if you have exceeded the permitted number of words, prune it of unnecessary words and phrases that you might have used and bring it to the required length. Now go through it carefully to correct any mistakes that you might have made and to make sure that you have not left out any idea that is in the original. You can rest assured that your précis is good if the language you have used is comprehensible to a high school student – that is the touchstone of your précis. Now you can take a printout of the fair copy under the heading that you have given.

Although, as stated above, there is a vast difference between a précis and an abstract, if précis writing is practised, there will be no difficulty in writing the abstract of an article but not *vice versa*. So it is better to practise précis writing, for apart from preparing abstracts, the librarian may have to write short summaries of articles to help the clientele. The length of a précis has to be exactly a third of the original but an abstract should be much shorter, consisting of a few words. An abstract, unlike a précis, has to be classified and indexed, giving also bibliographical particulars about the passage that has been summarised. Various publications like journals, monographs, and books in all subjects as well as reports of committees and conferences are pouring out of the press in tens of thousands today; hence the need for abstracts. The purpose of abstracts is to enable research scholars, journalists and authors to trace easily the publications and the articles that are of interest to them.

An abstract, as stated above, is much – very much – shorter than a précis, comprising usually the keywords. It may be defined as the *minimal* outline of a book or a paper in a periodical, classified and indexed, giving necessary bibliographical particulars to help a person know the scope of the document abstracted and find the publication in which it appears. An abstract comprises three parts: (a) the subject heading or classification number, (b) the indexing entry and (c) the condensation of the original matter. Any of the various schemes of classification may be adopted for classifying the abstracts but many of the abstracting journals devise their own systems, for they find all the existing classification systems inadequate to meet their requirements. The indexing entry gives the title, the author and collaborator(s) if any, the bibliographical data, which includes the title of the journal, volume and issue numbers, date of the issue and the pages on which the original appears. The example of an abstract of a scientific paper quoted below (Indian, 2003) would give an idea as to how it is written:

C20 Desai, C.P.; Trivedi, J.C.; Patel, Arun A.; Mahesh, R. (Gujarat Agricultural University, Ahmedabad (India), Directorate of Extension Education) (2001) **A test to measure the knowledge level of mango orchard growers about drip irrigation system,**

Gujarat Agricultural University Research Journal (India), (July 1998) v. 24(1) p. 58-61 KEYWORDS: FARMERS; MANGOES; ORCHARDS; TRICKLE; IRRIGATION; INNOVATION ADOPTION 001

In the above abstract you find the following particulars: subject heading, author(s), year of publication, title, source, keywords; organisation under the auspices of which the work was carried out and the entry number in the abstracting journal. According to the classification followed by them, the subject heading C20 is 'Extension Work'. An article that appeared in four pages of the journal has been condensed into seven lines or 56 words that include all particulars mentioned above, regarding the paper. The whole matter of the articles is given in just twenty-two words including its title. These, the title and the keywords, will help the scholar to decide if the study presented in this article has any bearing on the investigation that he is carrying out. And if he thinks it does, he can easily retrieve it.

In the parliament/legislative assembly library, the elected members as well as the bureaucrats may come seeking information related to the subject of a Bill under discussion. They, naturally, may not have the time to search for the books and journals containing the information; it is for the librarian to look for and give it to them. The librarian may even have to take down notes from these books and periodicals and give to those who have asked for them. Similarly, an efficient librarian of the Bar council/court library, will rise to the occasion and help members of the bench and the bar retrieve from the myriad law journals and books, the precedents or some amendment(s) to the Act pertaining to a civil or criminal suit that is being argued in the court. In order to make the facilitation work easy the librarian should prepare abstracts of all articles in the law journals that are being subscribed to by the library. As abstracts are usually indexed and filed, there will be no need to go through the back numbers of all the journals to trace the required reference.

4
Reference Service

No one can claim that he or she knows all that is to be known even in the discipline in which he/she has made a specialised study, for in these days all fields of knowledge have been expanding at an incredible rate. All the knowledge gained is also recorded to be disseminated and these records, both printed and electronic, are being produced *pari passu* with the continually burgeoning knowledge. So writers, scholars, teachers and educatees may have to turn to this recorded knowledge for getting information that they are unaware of. Not many, however, know the various sources from which they can get whatever information they want in any discipline but they do know that those sources can be had from the library. Many of the enquirers go to the library, blindly look through all kinds of books, not knowing the exact source from which they can get the information. A few, however, stumble upon the correct sources. The rest, a vast majority of the enquirers, naturally approach the librarian in charge of reference service, that is the reference librarian, for help – evidently because they are not sure of the source from which they can get the information or to save time. No reference librarian would know everything under the sun – the enquirer who approaches him for the information also knows that the reference librarian does not know the answer to his query – but the enquirer hopes that the librarian, being a resource person, will be able to find out the information that he is seeking. And his hopes are seldom belied; the librarian usually finds out the information that the enquirer wants.

So everyone expects the librarian to know the various sources of information. A good reference librarian aims at becoming "a literature specialist, not a subject specialist. His aim should be to know about literature so that he can locate information himself or assist the user in finding information, whatever may be necessary." (Krishan Kumar, 1984). The librarian does know of course, myriad sources of information, books and periodicals being the traditional and the most common sources. There are many books, which are, so to speak, storehouses of information and these books, which are repositories of data, are not meant to be read but only to be referred and are called reference books. And reference service is the help that the librarian renders, voluntarily or if asked for, to an enquirer to retrieve either from the resources available in the library or from any source outside the library, the information being sought by the enquirer in person, by telephone, by e-mail or by any other means.

The word, *refer*, means "to turn for information or help" and *reference* means "something used for information or help". Students often refer to a dictionary, which is a book of reference. According to the American Library Association, a reference book is that in which the topics are arranged and treated in such a way that it is meant only to be consulted and used strictly within the precincts of the library. Every librarian should be familiar with various reference books; he should know what each of them contains and how to find the information from it. Of these reference books, the most frequently used ones are dictionaries and encyclopaedias. The dictionary of course, is the most widely used reference book – the one reference book that is frequently used even by children. By the time children come to class five, or perhaps even earlier, they are introduced to the dictionary. The language teacher insists on their referring to the dictionary whenever they find a word of which the meaning is not known to them and thus instils the 'dictionary habit' in them. Anyway, it is only the children's librarian who may occasionally find the necessity to help readers consult dictionaries.

The term *dictionary* is commonly used to denote a book that explains the words in general or some special kind of words of a language and is usually arranged in alphabetical order. A bilingual dictionary like a Sanskrit – Malayalam dictionary, on the other hand, gives the equivalent Malayalam words for Sanskrit words, arranged in alphabetical order. The most well-known lexicon in Sanskrit is *Amarakosa* by Amarasimha, in versified form but the words are not in alphabetical order as dictionaries are designed today. It is believed to have been composed about 500 AD. Purushothamadeva's *Trikanda-sesha,* composed, perhaps about 1300 AD is a supplement to it. *Anekartha samuchaya* by Sasvata is said to have been composed prior to *Amarakosa* and Halayudha's *Abhidhanaratnamala*, in *circa* 950 AD. There are a few more dictionaries in Sanskrit, of which Yadavaprakasa's *Vyjayanti* (10th century AD), Mahesvara Kavi's *Visvaprakasa* (1111 AD), four dictionaries, one each of synonyms, homonyms, Prakrit and botanical terms, composed by Hemachandra between 1088 and 1172 AD are noteworthy (Macdonnel, A.A., 1971). Though not the first, Samuel Johnson's *A Dictionary of the English Language*, published in 1755 is a landmark in the history of English lexicography. He also collaborated with Dr. Robert James in producing a *Medicinal Dictionary*. However, the earliest known dictionary was the one to the works of Homer and the earliest Greek dictionary, which was arranged according to the meanings of words is known to have been compiled in the 2nd century AD.

But there are dictionaries other than those explaining the meanings of words. There are, for example, Dictionary of Biographies, which is a book wherein accounts of the lives of people are given, usually arranged in alphabetical order, Dictionary of Dates, Dictionary of Artists and many like those, dealing with various subjects although the word 'dictionary' brings to our mind only the dictionary to which we usually refer to find meanings of words. So a dictionary can be a book of information on any branch of knowledge wherein items are arranged in a specified order, usually alphabetical and is meant to be for reference only. These dictionaries are very similar to encyclopaedias, not general but specialised. Strangely, although there were dictionaries, no encyclopaedias as such had been found in Sanskrit. Encyclopaedia is a product of Greek civilisation, the oldest one that can be called by that name being the *Natural History* compiled by Pliny the Elder, in the 8th century AD. The title is misleading because apart from science, it includes subjects like geography, arts and medicine. In fact, the word *encyclopaedia* is derived from the Greek word, *enkyklios paldela*, meaning "well-rounded education" which presupposes the range of knowledge it is expected to cover. Today, however, there are general encyclopaedias, like the *Encyclopaedia Britannica* for example, that deal with different subjects and specialised encyclopaedias, like for instance the *Encyclopaedia of Library and Information Science*, that confine themselves to a particular field of knowledge. Many a reader, young or old, student or scholar may not know which reference book to look into to find the right answer to the question he has in mind. So they naturally approach the librarian who, they are confident, would not disappoint them. .

Apart from dictionaries and encyclopaedias there are various other reference books also. Gazetteers, Almanacs, Yearbooks, Who's Whos, Atlases, Road Maps, Time Tables of Railways and Buses are a few of them and all of these, except gazetteers are annual publications. Let us just flip the pages of each of these to know what they contain, how the matter in each of them is arranged and the area of knowledge that each covers. It is necessary for the librarian to have a clear idea of all these reference books, without which, if an enquirer seeks his help, he would be helpless and cut a sorry figure. The reference section of every library should be the strongest, stocked with all kinds of reference books, general and specialised.

Well, to return to reference books: gazetteers are very useful for finding out details about a city, town, port or any place, ancient or modern. Usually arranged in alphabetical order of the names of places or could be first arranged by countries and then by place names, gazetteers may show the location, geography, demographics, exports, agriculture, industries and perhaps give a brief history and such other details of places. *The Imperial Gazetteer of India* by W.W.Hunter is a very good example. The almanacs, which are an annual publication, are generally considered nothing more than a calendar that, in addition, gives information about the weather, tides, sun, moon, planetary positions, stars, religious holidays (depending on which religious society or group publishes it) and such other facts. But there is the reference book called the 'almanac' that includes information on various other subjects apart from those mentioned above. An example of such an almanac is *Whitaker's Almanack*, which is virtually a mine of information, covering almost all spheres of human activity. It is an excellent book of reference although very much UK biased. There is *Almanac de Gotha*, which may be called international. It confines itself mainly to the ruling class and political developments of all nations. Yearbooks, an example of which is *Manorama Yearbook*, also would cover a wide ground encompassing geographical, historical and economic facts about all the countries of the world. It would also give statistical information, brief biographical sketches of people who had distinguished themselves during the year, lists of Nobel Laureates, Arjuna Awardees, recipients of

Booker Prizes and such other facts too. If anyone wants addresses of foreign embassies in India, they can refer to any of the Yearbooks published in the country. Who's Whos, Atlases, Road Maps, and Time Tables of Railways/buses do not need any explanation. There are many other reference books, for example Directories like the Telephone Directory or the Trade Directory and such others, which most people are quite familiar with and generally no one goes to the library to refer to them because the persons concerned would be having copies of those publications.

A librarian to be a successful information retriever has to be well informed of not only the reference books that have been discussed but also all the reference and non-reference books in his library. In fact, even that is not enough. There could be many other titles that are as good as or even better than what we have just discussed or what there are in the library over which he presides. The librarian should know in general what those publications have to offer and if they are in any library in the town. Some of those may be in the local college or polytechnic institute library. So librarians of all libraries that are in a town must know the resources of neighbourhood libraries and if an enquirer fails to find what he wants in the reference books that are in one library, the librarian concerned may give him a referral to the librarian of the library where the reference book in which the required information could be found, is. Incidentally, making the readers run from library to library in search of a small piece of information blatantly violates one of the cardinal principles of the philosophy of library service, which is to make it as simple and easy as possible for readers to avail of the resources of the library and to provide them with the maximum facilities to study and research. Needless to say, inter-linking of libraries or at least introduction of inter-library loan system would obviate this difficulty for the reader because then he would not have to run to the other library for the information that he wanted.

There could be many queries for which answers could be found in books that are in the lending section of the library but the enquirer, not knowing that, approaches the librarian for help. In fact, certain topics are discussed in greater detail and by a more distinguished authority in those books than in any of the reference books, including those exclusively devoted to the subject concerned. A good librarian would generally know not only the contents of all such books in the library but also the relative value of those books.

In a small or medium-sized library, it is not very difficult for the librarian to be familiar with and even remember all the books. Besides, such a library would naturally be in a village or a small town, the clientele of which would usually be a homogeneous group known to the librarian. So the possible queries would be somewhat similar and confined to certain areas of knowledge only, depending upon the professional or vocational pattern of the population. This makes it easy for the librarian to deal with queries because he can, to some extent, surmise the areas of knowledge from which information would be sought and even the type of queries; hence the librarian has to be conversant with the books in those disciplines only. And that may not be much. But in a city where the library is big, with myriad books in all subjects and a disparate clientele, the situation is different. The collection being so large, it is quite difficult for a person to know and remember the contents of all the books even in one discipline unless he has a Gargantuan memory. To add to the problem, the clientele being heterogeneous the queries that might come up could be anybody's guess and so it is not possible to anticipate the type of queries or foresee even the area of knowledge from which the reader may want the information. But whether the library is in the rural or urban area, whether the circle of users is small or big, whether the collection is large or small, without proper preparation, the reference librarian will be at a loss when an enquirer seeks his help. And if the librarian does prepare, it may not be difficult for him to retrieve any information, howsoever huge the collection is.

A good teacher never steps into a class without preparing the lesson thoroughly; nor would a conscientious Minister attend a parliamentary session without doing proper 'home work'. Even if C.V.Raman had been asked to give a talk on Raman Effect, it is quite unlikely that he would have spoken off the cuff. But in all these cases, they know what to prepare. The teacher knows the lesson that she is going to teach and can prepare that. The minister knows the questions that would come up on each day and can be thorough with those problems. And C.V.Raman knew that he had to speak on Raman Effect and could prepare his talk for the day. However, the audiences are not aware of the hard work put in by these people behind the screen, as it were. It is essentially on account of the preparation done earlier that a teacher becomes a *good* teacher and a minister becomes a *conscientious* minister. The *profundity* of a speech given by any speaker is also the result of the preparation that he makes beforehand. In short, any intellectual work needs sufficient preparation and few realise that reference service is an intellectual work, although it does not seem so. And so, if the reference librarian has to be good at fact-finding, he should put in continual hard work; there is no other way. He may be an authority in a particular subject or he may be a well-known writer but that will not make him a good reference librarian. A reference librarian has to be a 'jack of all subjects' and need not be a master of any. Whenever he gets free time, no successful reference librarian would sit back and be woolgathering; he knows that it is the time for him to prepare and not to relax.

How and what does he prepare when he does not know

what information the next enquirer or subsequent enquirers would be wanting? The preparation that the reference librarian is expected to make is called 'Shelf Study'. He goes round the shelves, picks up at random any informational book and skims through it; keeps it back and picks up some other book and glances thorough it – he goes on like that looking though many books. In a day, he may thus be covering quite a few books. He does not necessarily be studying the reference books alone; he may pick up books from the lending section in the library and browse, reading snatches from them. But he is not satisfied; he does not think that now he knows the contents of those books thoroughly. Day after day, he does the same work, going through perhaps the same books. Incidentally, shelf study also helps him find misplaced books and he puts them back in their proper places. Apart from scanning the books that are on the shelves, he must pay special attention to abstracting journals and even unpublished materials like doctoral theses, mimeographed reports and such others. His intention is not to augment his knowledge of any subject or to read for pleasure. If he is interested in recreational reading or in reading a book on any subject, he can borrow the book that he wants and read at home. In the library, he is on duty and whatever time he gets has to be devoted to his work as librarian. Shelf study is an essential duty of a reference librarian – rather all librarians. A librarian who regularly and continually makes shelf study would remember not only the contents of books and their call numbers but even the colour of the cover and the size of each of those books as well. He will also know where, in which bookcase and in which bay, a particular book is. And it will remain in his memory for years to come!

An important retrieval tool that would immensely help the reference librarian is the abstracting journal. Several abstracting journals are being brought out by various organisations. In the previous chapter, 'Facilitation' we have seen an example of an entry in *The Indian Agricultural Sciences Abstracts* (IASA) that The Indian Council of Agricultural Research brings out. There are highly acclaimed abstracting journals like the *Current Contents* (CC), *Science Citation Index* (SCI), *Index Chemicus* (IC) and several similar publications that every special or university library must subscribe to. Abstracting journals will be an asset even in libraries of colleges that have students working for doctorate degrees, for as is symbolically stated in the Foreword of IASA of February 2003, the up-to-date information that abstracting journals provide, would make "re-invention of wheels" unnecessary. And subscribing to an abstracting journal is equivalent to getting hundreds of learned journals. The CC covers biological and physical Sciences, Education and Behavioural Sciences as well as Social and Management Sciences. The SCI is said to provide access to information from not less than 3,00,000 current source articles per year and bibliographic information on several million cited books and journal articles. And Index Chemicus reports on nearly 2,00,000 newly synthesised chemicals each year. Needless to say, abstracting journals like these would be of great help to reference librarians, not to speak of research scholars.

All libraries – public, academic (including schools that have reasonably good libraries) and special – procure a large number of periodicals, most of which contain valuable articles that could be of use to the intellectual section of the clientele, though not immediately, some time later. All those magazines may not be worth preserving. Some of them may be trash; some of them may carry articles of ephemeral value only. Some magazines may have a few articles that deserve to be preserved; those may be clipped and filed. Such articles may be seen in newspapers also; they too have to be clipped and filed. But there are magazines carrying articles of lasting value – magazines like *The Economic and Political Weekly* and even *Frontline*. These are to be preserved *in toto*. These and similar magazines are to be bound and kept in the library, with the result over the years, naturally they accumulate. When an enquirer seeks some information and even if that person says that he/she remembers having read it a few weeks or months back in one of those magazines it is quite difficult to go through all the back numbers searching for it. Except perhaps special libraries and university libraries, usually no other type of library subscribes to abstracting journals. And no abstracting journals cover the magazines usually subscribed to by the other types of libraries. But most articles published in some of those magazines may be of lasting value and someone or the other may want to refer to any of those articles at a later date. So it is incumbent upon the reference librarian to abstract them. These abstracts may be classified, indexed and filed to facilitate the reader to retrieve any article without difficulty. The reader will not have the trouble of flipping the pages of hundreds of back numbers of a magazine to find the article(s) containing the information that he wants; instead he can go through the abstract files and trace the issue or issues of the magazine(s) containing the information. These abstract files will be of use not only to the readers but to the reference librarian, as well.

One important source of information is the bibliography, which is a very useful tool for the reference librarian as well as the scholar. The bibliography gives all the particulars of each of the books listed therein: the author, title, publisher, year of publication, edition, illustrated or not, the scope of the book and even details of the format. In short, it would contain all the particulars necessary for the reference librarian to find out which book would have the information that precisely answers a scholar's query. It is useful for the scholar too as it gives what he would like to know about each book on the subject listed in it, so that he can decide what book would serve his purpose.

There are, however, different types of bibliographies like, for example, comprehensive, basic, special and select. The comprehensive bibliography attempts to compile all sorts of reading materials on a subject up to a certain year while the basic one includes only, though all, the fundamental works in a subject up to a certain date. The special bibliography confines itself to a particular author or a subject or a narrow branch of knowledge. The select bibliography, as the name indicates is selective in the choice of books included, for it lists only the highly rated books or books suited to a special purpose. All these may be quite useful for the reference librarian. If the query is of a general nature by a layman, the first one is the best to refer to while if the information is required by a research scholar, any of the other three bibliographies, depending on the query, would be ideal. In addition to these, there are retrospective and current bibliographies. The first one, obviously, is a list of documents published in the past on a subject, brought up to a certain year but there may be annual supplements to it. The current bibliography, needless to say, is a list of the current literature. Whatever type it is, a bibliography is a reliable guide to the literature of any discipline that helps find out materials on a subject. And as Lloyd puts it, a bibliography is "aimed at the librarian, the general scholar and the layman requiring data on a subject." (Lloyd, 1965.)

Many countries in the world are bringing out national bibliographies, which are prepared either by the national library of the country concerned or by national bibliographic institutes. In our country, in the absence of a national bibliographic institute, the responsibility for bringing out a national bibliography lies with the National Library in Kolkata covering all books published in the country in English as well as in all the languages recognised by our

Constitution under Schedule VIII. An 'authoritative bibliographical record of current Indian publications' the national bibliography is expected to include all the books sent to the National Library by the publishers in the country, as mandated by the Delivery of Books and Newspapers Act, 1954 (and amended in 1956). The Indian National Scientific Documentation Centre, New Delhi prepares and supplies, on request, bibliography of recent papers published on any scientific topic and responds to technical enquiries of informative nature. The Defence Scientific Information and Documentation Centre, New Delhi brings out current and retrospective bibliographies besides providing bibliographies on specific topics if asked for. Similarly, bibliographies of specialised type are being brought out by various organisations in our country. The Bhabha Atomic Research Centre, Mumbai, provides bibliographical services in nuclear science and the National Medical Library, New Delhi, in medical science. The latter also brings out the *Index to Indian Medical Periodicals*. Bibliographies, however, would not provide the information that the enquirer seeks but only the source(s) in which the information could be found.

If the librarian fails to find the answer to an enquirer's query from reference books or any printed document whatsoever, nowadays he collects information from non-printed materials, of which the source that gives the latest information is the Internet. We get any information on the Internet much before it comes in the periodicals, which had been the source of latest information prior to the advent of the Internet. The Internet, today, is an excellent source of information from where up-to-date developments in any field of knowledge can be had through the many search engines or the relevant web sites. So even if one wants to find any information on the Internet, he or she should know the right search engine – there are general, specialised and meta search engines that will help retrieve information on any subject – and/or the correct web site to go to. So if the librarian finds a reader fumbling at the computer, browsing at wrong Internet sites, he should tell him the most suitable search engine for his purpose and/or guide him to the right web site. The reference librarian, therefore, has to be conversant with all the search engines and know the various web site links.[1]

So every librarian, today, must be able to use the Internet as well as to help readers use the Internet, for which, first of all, he has to know what Internet is. Of course, if he has elementary knowledge of the computer, he would know that the Internet is a world-wide collection of interconnected networks. A network can be defined in simple terms as a series of interconnected points or in other words, it is the interconnection of a number of points by communications facilities. From the perspective of a librarian, it is a group of computers that are connected together to share resources. And in libraries in the developed countries, the network usually shares printers and also shows the reader a variety of databases.

Prior to the advent of computers, various reference books mentioned above were the main sources of information and periodicals had been the source of latest information on any topic. But once libraries are automated, the librarian has the responsibility of encouraging the users to use Internet for getting latest information on any subject. This does not mean that reference books and periodicals have lost their value as sources of information and are obsolescent. Certainly, not. However, several encyclopaedias and periodicals can be accessed on-line now, although some of them are to be subscribed to. In fact, since the establishment of World Wide Web, commonly known by its abbreviation WWW or The Web, the information retrieval service of Internet, has replaced periodicals as the chief source of latest information. This helps users access a vast collection of documents, which are interconnected by means of hypermedia links. These links connect various bits of related information so that, users have easy access to them. But quite a few of the users may not be computer literates and so until such time that most people are able to use the computer it may be necessary for the reference librarian himself to get the information from the Internet. Or, he has to teach those who are not computer savvy, how to go on to the Internet and retrieve the required information. This problem, however, will be faced mostly by librarians of schools or juvenile and adult public libraries because the clientele of the other types of libraries are expected to be well conversant with computers.

The librarian, particularly the reference librarian, as stated above, must be a 'jack of all subjects'. It is not necessary for him to read intensively and be a scholar in any subject but he must read extensively, covering various subjects, just to have a general idea of all subjects. This is desirable because as reference librarian, the queries that he gets from readers may be varied, pertaining to different subjects depending on the area of interest of the reader concerned. Only if the librarian is familiar with all the subjects would he be able to figure out what exactly the reader is asking for and find the information that the enquirer wants or direct him to the source that gives the right answer to his query.

A good reference librarian, on principle, responds with alacrity to the queries of all readers, irrespective of the person's age, sex, religion, creed, race, colour, or standing in society, with due respect. And he responds with equal respect to their queries whether he is a well-known author, a research scholar, a local political activist, a high official, a desultory reader, an occasional visitor, a child or even a stranger who is not a member of the library. In other words, he treats all enquirers alike, without any discrimination whatsoever. And he, treats all queries as strictly confidential, attends to those queries with the same seriousness of purpose and ensures that he makes every effort to get the information asked for.

It is important that the reference librarian has to be a person of immense patience, even temper, genial temperament, and who is capable of handling more than one enquirer simultaneously without getting flustered. He must be able to build up a good rapport with all readers and must be specially considerate to the physically challenged. He has to be physically fit, for on certain days he may have to be on his toes all the time, with no time to relax. He should listen to the enquirer patiently and sympathetically and try to grasp what exactly his requirement is. At times the enquirer could be vague and may not be very precise in explaining what exactly he wants, in which case the reference librarian has to elicit from him the information he needs by *tactfully* questioning him.

McColvin mentions in his book that one library has issued a small poster with the words, "Whenever you want to know anything ask the Public Library to help you". Copies of this have been sent to all offices and works in the town to be displayed on their notice boards (McColvin, 1933). This is a good idea. In addition to that, such a poster may be projected on the screen in all local cinema theatres along with advertisement strips. The theatre owners, all of whom or at least a representative of theirs would be on The Public Library Extension Service Committee (details of which shall be discussed in the next chapter, 'Extension Service'), may do this free of charge, if requested. Academic and special libraries may put up such posters on all the notice boards in the building and also in front of the library.

Footnotes

1 Please see Appendix 1 for a selected list of Internet sites.

5
Extension Service

Most people regard library merely as a centre for reading periodicals, which they visit to glance through daily newspapers and current magazines or at the most, a centre for recreational reading providing them with books of fiction. A few like, for example, those who want to improve their professional skill or educational qualifications consider it a centre for self-education while some who are interested in researching, however, look upon the library as a resource centre – which a good library, today, is – and make use of it for investigative reading. Strangely, no one thinks of the library as an institution that has been entrusted by the community with the task of spearheading the movement for the social and cultural upliftment of the illiterate masses because in the perception of the common man, the library is still just a collection of books and periodicals to be made use of by literate persons only.

The librarian cannot close his eyes to the stark reality that there is a large section of society steeped in illiteracy, unable to make use of the library services, thanks to the economic system and the resultant stratified social structure. As such, the library in a democratic society, is not or ought not to be, what it had been hitherto – it cannot just keep its doors open for the privileged class, comprising the educatees, the educands, the educated, the literate sections of the community, to step in and utilise its resources and services. In our Constitution, Art. 29 (2), Part III – Fundamental Rights, it is stated that "No citizen shall be denied admission into any educational institution maintained by the State or receiving aid out of State funds on grounds only of religion, race, caste, language or any of them." The library is nothing but an educational institution to which the underprivileged that forms a large section of our society is not, by law, denied admission. But because of its penurious condition it is deprived of the opportunity for education, consequent upon which it is unable to make use of the library, which is virtually an educational institution. In effect this amounts to denial of admission into an educational institution, the public library, that is maintained by the State. So if what is guaranteed in our Constitution is to be meaningful, all those illiterate men, women and children also must be able to take advantage of the educational facilities that the library offers.

In order, therefore, to make it possible for them to take advantage of library facilities, the library has to reach out to the very periphery of the society that this section occupies. It is in extending the services to the marginalised section of the population that the library movement in our country – rather, in most countries – has been guilty of neglecting so far. The library is, thus, something more than a magazine centre, more than a recreation centre, more than a centre for self-education, more than a resource centre for researching, in short, much more than an institution rendering passive service to the literate and the educated few. It is a proactive centre of extension service, which is different from the traditional extension service that libraries usually undertake. This, in other words, is social service. But the social service that the library is expected to carry out is not mere cosmetic action like, once in a while distributing some clothes to a few slum dwellers, supplying food packets gratis to the hungry masses, sweeping and cleaning the premises of the huts of the poor or conducting night classes for the illiterate children and adults as many of the social service organisations do. What they are doing is, no doubt, commendable and a great help to those who do not have the basic necessities of life. But the librarian has to keep in mind that the library as social service centre has a commitment to the cause of the under-privileged and social service is carried out with the objective of improving them educationally and culturally while encouraging them to assert themselves. So the social service that the librarian renders in the form of literacy and adult education classes for the culturally deprived segment of the population, must go much deeper than those carried out by the various social service organisations. We shall discuss this in detail a little later.

It is to this economically backward segment of the community, which so far lay outside the jurisdiction of library services, that library services are necessarily to be extended. And that is to be done through literacy and adult education classes. Many librarians may say that the task of spreading literacy and education among the marginalized, falls within the purview of the social welfare department and is not the responsibility of the library. They forget that all types of libraries, including the public library, are an institution of informal education and the public library is what may be called a 'People's University'. As such it is an instrument of social welfare. It cannot, therefore, absolve itself of the responsibility for undertaking social service schemes with an educational thrust and the social service that the library does is nothing but extension service. In fact, the literacy and adult education classes that the library must conduct in slum areas and other centres outside the premises of the library, may be regarded as an activity akin to the programme, known as 'Distance Education' that most universities today have been conducting. The universities, today, regard it as an essential part of their function, which the revolutionary changes in educational technology brought about by the galloping developments in electronics have made it easy to be executed. The same educational technology would facilitate the extension of the traditional frontiers of library service to encompass the segment of the community that so far lay beyond it.

The section of the community to be covered by this extension service must include the illiterate masses of both sexes of all ages, the lumpen youth, the school dropouts, the prisoners, the in-patients, the physically challenged and all those who have hitherto been denied the benefit of library services. The librarian has to realise that a library is judged by the services it renders, not just to the educated, the literate and even the neo-literate section of the society but to the illiterates, the disabled and the culturally deprived masses as well. Today, however, librarians, library authorities and educationists are ensconced in an ivory tower and do not see the multitude existing beyond the educated and literate sections of society. It must be understood that services for the underprivileged are not solely the responsibility of the public library. In a country like ours, where illiterates far outnumber literates and neo-literates put together, the public library alone cannot do much in relating library to the masses; academic libraries comprising the school, college and university libraries too have to share the burden, not excepting, of course, the Departments of Education and Social Welfare.

In fact, the adult education campaign launched in 1948 and the National Adult Education Programme of 1978 did not achieve much because the library was kept out of the Movements. The National Literacy Mission too seems to have ignored the library. It must be understood that in any Movement connected with literacy and/or education, library is an important tool and can play a decisive role. Apart from it, unless the library is equipped with books meant for neo-literates whatever literacy has been achieved, cannot be sustained; the neo-literates are bound to relapse into illiteracy in the absence of suitable reading materials and the necessary arrangements to provide them with those reading materials. It is imperative, therefore, that the public library has proper primers for illiterates and other necessary instructional materials to back up these programmes as well as reading materials for neo-literates. The Education and Social Welfare departments of the respective States that are engaged in fighting illiteracy and ignorance should consider the library as their base camp, while the librarian in turn must support and co-operate without any reservation the government departments in their campaign against illiteracy and ignorance. In short, the public library should be the underprop of any literacy and education schemes.

But independent of all that the government departments as well as local social service organisations do in this sphere, the public library should spearhead the struggle against illiteracy, educational backwardness and ignorance. The number of professionals and non-professionals manning public libraries today is quite inadequate to carry out the suggested extension service, as some of the personnel will have to work till late in the evening. An increase in the strength of the library staff is, therefore, a prerequisite for undertaking this service. Presuming that the library would be open from 8 a.m. to 11 p.m. as it is under the 'Swiss-American system', which was discussed earlier in Chapter 1, 'Librarianship in India', one batch of staff can be on duty from eight O'clock in the morning to 3.30 in the afternoon. And the next batch can take over for the next seven and a half hours. The second batch that takes over will have to carry out the extension service and so there should be more number of persons on duty in the second batch, as some will have to go for extension service. The section of the community that is targeted by the extension service will be back at their homes after work mostly by late evening. And after the routine household chores and meals, they would be free for the class not earlier than 8 O'clock on any day.

However, literacy classes for their children can be conducted before that, for they would be at home much earlier.

The increase in the strength of the staff does not do away with the necessity to work in tandem with various Non-Government Organisations (NGOs), if the library decides to extend its jurisdiction of services to the entire community, instead of the privileged minority, which alone comes under its umbrella now. The public librarian has to realise that the extension service, as stated earlier, is similar to the Distance Education Programmes being conducted by universities and cannot be carried out by the library on its own. The Directorate of Distance Education is funded by the university concerned and is a separate unit as such, with a strong contingent of teaching and administrative staff. Public libraries cannot expect to have a wing with the required staff solely to carry out the extension service; it has to find people who are prepared to take these evening classes as a labour of love. Hence, it is necessary to seek the co-operation and support of all the libraries in the town, the NGOs and even some influential individuals in the community, for there could be many among them who are service-minded and are willing to volunteer their services.

Who will finance the project? The envisaged extension service cannot be carried out without a mobile unit – a large vehicle, somewhat like a large house trailer, fitted with shelves for keeping books and a small cupboard for keeping a ledger and other non-book materials connected with the service, with seating accommodation for at least two persons, a library assistant and an attendant, at the back. Near the rear door like that of the police van, there should be a small counter. In the front, by the side of the driver there will be space for three persons and that will accommodate the librarian and the two volunteers. This – purchasing and altering a vehicle to meet these specific requirements – is a capital investment, involving a huge sum of money. Besides, the targeted segment of the community has to be supplied with books and pencils and the library has to provide itself with a blackboard and boxes of chalk, all of which will be a recurring expenditure. The librarian will have to coax the NGOs to fund this programme, for no governmental aid for it can be expected.

In order to get such co-operation and support the public librarian has to be good at public relations. When it is said that the librarian has to be good at public relations, it means that he should have much more interpersonal skill to deal with and win the favour of the VIPs of the community than in dealing with the clientele and staff of the library. It is, therefore, of paramount importance that the librarian has to be a person who is able to deal with all sorts of people. Suffice it to say here, the warmth that the librarian exudes should make it easy for him to interact with various agencies that might be of help in the extension service that the library intends to carry out for the educational and cultural upliftment of the masses.

What are the NGOs that should necessarily be cultivated? That the public library on its own steam cannot carry out this task has been pointed out earlier. No public library has the manpower and the infrastructure, let alone the funds, required for such social work and hence the help and co-operation of organisations and individuals interested in or have a stake in social work have to be sought. The organisations that must inevitably be contacted are the Municipal Council/Village Panchayat, political parties, trade unions and local social service organisation(s), for they may already be in touch with this section of the community. Besides, teachers' unions, parent-teacher associations, women's organisation(s), the Rotary Club, Lions Club, Round Table – in short all such secular organisations could also be profitably made use of in this work. Apart from these, it is necessary to involve librarians of all the libraries – academic and special, if there are any – in the locality, individuals like the local MP, MLA, and any prominent and influential persons of the locality, in this activity. The librarian should not ignore officials like the District Collector, District Educational Officer, Superintendent of Police, Block Development Officer and any other important officials in the town/village; they too must be contacted and their help solicited. The Office bearers of all these NGOs, government officials and individuals would of course be preoccupied with their own activities or official duties. True; but on certain days some of them will be free from their regular activities and many of them, particularly those connected with the various non-government organisations mentioned above would only be happy to lend a helping hand if approached. So the librarian has to be in close touch with them to find out who all would be free and when and arrange literacy or adult education classes to suit their conveniences.

In order to function smoothly, the librarian should constitute a committee, which may be called 'The Public Library Extension Service Committee'. This is necessary to bring together the different organisations and to get the necessary funds for carrying out the service. The committee may comprise the secretaries of all those organisations or any member deputed by the secretary of the organisation concerned, the MP and the MLA of the constituency and one or two influential individuals in the town/village and inevitably the librarians of all types of libraries in the locality. Obviously, therefore, certain members of the committee may change depending on who the secretaries of those organisations are and the librarian may also change the individuals not connected with any of these organisations. So at the time of nominating them, they must be told that the term of membership is one year, except of course the librarians who will be on the committee permanently to be replaced by the new incumbent, if any one is transferred.

The meetings may be chaired by each of the members in rotation according to the alphabetical order of the names of the committee members. It will have an honorary secretary, elected for a term of one year from among the members of the committee, with the public librarian as *ex-officio* convenor. It should meet in the first week of every month on a day convenient to the members and at each meeting the date for the subsequent meeting may be fixed after ascertaining the convenience of the majority of the members. It is desirable to draw up a constitution for the committee incorporating all these points as well as its powers and functions to avoid any problem arising in the future. Nevertheless, the public librarian being the convenor should not fail to remind each member about the meeting, at least four to five days in advance, by e-mail, regular post or phone, preferably one of the former. To make this easy, a letter of intimation may be printed on postcards, a specimen format for which is given below (see fig. 1).

Fig. 1

Specimen format for the reminder.

The Public Library Extension Service Committee

(Name of the town or village)

Dear Mr./Ms.,

This is to remind you that the next meeting of the Committee will be held at the Public Library on ——— 200 , at ——— a.m./p.m., as decided upon at the last meeting held on ———, 200 . Your presence is requested.

Agenda:

1. ....
2. ....
3. ....

  * ....
  * ....

Thank you.

Librarian

Convenor

Date:

The public librarian as the convenor has to make the necessary arrangements for the meetings and it is better that he, if the secretary agrees, writes the minutes of the meetings. The minutes must contain a true account of what transpired at the meeting, a gist of the discussions and the decisions taken besides the follow up action taken by the librarian on the decisions taken at the previous meeting.

The committee has three important functions. (i) At the monthly meetings it has to review the work done earlier and chart out the programme for the current month. The librarian may put up the account – the expenditure incurred in the previous month and the budget for the current month – and get it approved by the committee. (ii) It has to find two volunteers to accompany the librarian and his colleagues to help them conduct the literacy and adult education classes. (iii) Primarily, it has to fund the purchase of the vehicle and also build a corpus so that the interest that accrues on it will help meet the recurring expenditure. All the money collected should be deposited in a local bank in the name of The Public Library Extension Service Committee, to be operated jointly by the Secretary of the committee and the *ex-officio* Convenor of the committee. So once the committee is constituted and it starts functioning. the committee will fund and monitor the extension service, which will be planned and executed by the librarian.

As stated above, the extension (social) service that the librarian renders in the form of literacy and adult education classes must go much deeper than those carried out by the various social service organisations. So these classes are not just for teaching them to read and write. Cornforth writes, "The materialist doctrine that men are products of circumstances and upbringing and that, therefore, changed men are produced by changed circumstances and changed upbringing, forgets that circumstances are changed precisely by men and that the educator must himself be educated." (Cornforth, 1976.) Hence in these classes, the educator and the educatees, 'both learn, both question, both reflect and both participate in meaning-making.' The librarian should, therefore, bear in mind that although man is conditioned by the society of which he is a unit, he has the brains to appreciate it and decondition himself. He is capable of reconditioning the society as he wants it to be, and by conscious action, purge it of the features that impede his growth, in the process replacing them with favourable conditions that help the overall improvement of the society and of himself. In other words, the extension (social) service has to be cultural action aimed at developing in the oppressed critical consciousness that would help open their eyes to the social conditions that are inimical to their growth and to awaken their latent ability to replace those with conditions that are congenial to the all-round development of their personalities. To put it in simple terms, the education that is imparted to them must help them understand the reality that has caused their wretchedness and should give them the necessary self-confidence to transform the reality by eliminating altogether the root cause of their present plight. Literacy classes for the deprived children and adult education classes for the marginalised grown-ups are the means by which this could be achieved. As Freire points out, "Only someone with a mechanical mentality, which Marx would call 'grossly materialistic', could reduce adult literacy learning to a purely technical action" (Freire, 1977). First of all, the librarian has to ensure that these underprivileged men, women and children do not develop a sense of failure or a complex of defeatism. Hence, before actually getting into the process of teaching the alphabet, there has to be a few sessions of general education aimed at sensitisation. They must be made aware of the fact that education is an important weapon that would help them improve their lot and the library is the best means for him to educate himself once he acquires the ability to read and write. That will be an impetus for them to acquire literacy and educate themselves and if they are assured that the library is open to them, they would only be too happy to come to the library to educate themselves.

But they have always been looking at the library with awe considering it a place, which is out of bounds for them and they have no business to enter. And that has been a fact. A person from that stratum of society, an illiterate, has not been and still is not welcomed in any library. So even after they become literate, they may hesitate to enter the library. In order that they get rid of the phobia, occasionally a film show or some other programme like a puppet show or magic show, for example, must be arranged in the library hall and they must be invited for it. Initially, the librarian and one or two of the committee members who are familiar to them must go with the library vehicle and bring them to the library, for otherwise they may hesitate to come for the show. Two or three times if they are brought like that, then if they are informed of the programme and invited over, they would only be happy to come. And once the psychological barrier is removed, they must be encouraged to come into the library at any time. Apart from picture books, 'talking' books and simple storybooks written specifically for neo-literates, the library should have playthings, records, audiocassettes and discs with popular film songs and folk songs. These will be an added attraction for them, especially for their children, to visit the library occasionally, if not frequently. The NGO, like the social service organisations, international organisations like for example the Rotary Club and others may be requested to distribute clothes to these people, both adults and children, so that they do not develop inferiority complex when they come into the library, where they may find only well-dressed or neatly dressed people.

It is a good idea to organise occasionally, not less than twice in a year, 'Parents' Library Festival' and invite the parents of maginalised children. On this occasion, the library staff can take the parents round the library, show them the facilities that are available, explain to them the services that the library renders and urge them to persuade their children to come to the library as often as possible. They must be assured that the children are welcome to the library and that they will benefit by visiting the library. They will, then, prevail upon their children to visit the library. Incidentally, this will also help these adults overcome their hesitation to come into the library and in course of time, create library-consciousness in them. Similarly, 'Children's Library Festivals', targeting children of *all social classes*, may be held periodically. The invitees to this festival are only children and these festivals are intended to familiarise them with juvenile books. They may, therefore, be shown the books for neo-literates, picture books and such others meant for children of 4-12 age group, that are in the library and may also be told what type of stories are in them, picking up a few examples because there may not be time to introduce all the books. The festivals for the parents could be arranged in the afternoons but the children's festivals should be full day programmes. Notices to this effect should be put up on the library notice board, a week before these festivals. However, the library need not be closed for the others; one of the library personnel can attend to them.

At both these festivals, films may be screened. On the Parents' Library Festival day a documentary film and at the other, short films like *Cindrella, Aladdin and the Wonderful Lamp* or any animal stories, preferably the cartoon versions may be screened. Before starting each film, the librarian should give the children a gist of the story and show them the book in which the story appears. The librarian may also demonstrate the working of some of the mechanical and electronic toys and tell them, if they wish, to play for some time. They may also be told that whenever they come to the library they can play with all those toys. To ensure maximum attendance at the Parents' Library festivals, tea and light refreshments may be served to all invitees and on the Children's Library Festival day lunch too may be provided for all the invitees so that the children would remain there the whole day. The expenditure for these may be met from the committee's account and for this, prior permission of the committee may be taken at the meeting preceding each festival.

Festivals like the two mentioned above are equally, if not more, germane to the school library. However, instead of holding the library festival for *parents*, the school library will organise 'Mothers' Library Festival'. And this may be confined to the primary section. The purpose of this is not, as in the case of the marginalised children to acquaint the mothers with the facilities in the library and to advise them to persuade their children to visit the library, but to counsel them with the need to take more interest in their children's reading. Presuming that the mothers are educated, which they would usually be, in the case of most schools in urban areas and certain exclusive schools patronised by the affluent class, they may be told about the juvenile books, various types of which that are available in the market and the type that children of that age-group normally enjoy. And in one to one conference with each of those mothers, the librarian must discuss the child concerned – whether the child has developed reading interest, if so what his or her reading interests are or if not what remedial measures the librarian is taking and wishes the mother to take. All this will go a long way in fostering good relationship with the mothers of the little ones as well as in improving the reading habits of those kids. This opportunity could also be made use of to familiarise the children with the books in the library.

But most mothers – why, fathers too – of the children of schools in rural areas and even the parents of many of the lower and upper primary schools in the outskirts of towns, may be uneducated or first generation literates while quite a few could be even illiterate. They are therefore, not different from the parents of the marginalised children and so the library festival for them may be organised on the same lines as described earlier. So also the 'Children's Library Festival' in the case of the children of these schools. Of course, school library service is a privilege that most school children, especially primary school kids, in both urban and rural areas in our country do not enjoy. However, in certain States like Kerala, for example, there is practically no village or town that does not have a public library, some of which are well-stocked with books and may usually be subscribing to a variety of newspapers and magazines. So these public libraries, howsoever inadequately equipped they might be, must organise such festivals for the parents and children of the local or neighbourhood schools.

It is not easy to extend library service to the prisoners, for they cannot be brought to the library. So the librarian may have to go over to the prisons. The service to the prisoners is not different from that being rendered to the underprivileged adults. Many of the prisoners are usually illiterate and uneducated and so literacy and adult education classes are to be conducted for them, in the process conscientising them. First of all, they have to be made to understand that the prevailing socio-economic system which is responsible for the periodic economic recession and depression throwing hundreds of workers out of jobs and the consequent unemployment and poverty have driven them to do the illegal or criminal act for which they have been incarcerated. Basically none of them is a criminal. All are decent persons who would not have committed any of these crimes if they had the means of subsistence that has been denied to them by the society, which, in fact, is the real criminal. Bearing in mind that most prisoners, being usually from economically backward section of society, may be uneducated and even illiterate (not that those from affluent families and well-educated persons are not there; there could be quite a few but in their case, the reasons for committing the crimes may be different) the librarian has to convey the idea to them in simple terms. As stated above, both the educator and the educatees have to learn together, question together, reflect together and participate as a team in grasping the idea. Thus, the librarian has to first ensure that they shed their guilty conscience and try to instil a sense of pride in them before starting regular adult education classes. There could be some prisoners who would have had a little education and wanting to continue their studies. They could be helped by providing them with the required books pertaining to the syllabuses of whatever examinations they are interested in preparing for.

In the case of physically challenged persons and in-patients in hospitals also, the librarian has to take the books to them, for it will not be possible for them to come to the library. The school dropouts must be contacted with the help of school librarians or teachers. The public librarian along with the school librarian or the teacher concerned should visit them at their homes and request their parents to persuade their children to visit the library. This will help create in them an interest in reading. During those visits the librarian can talk to them and make them understand that they are welcome to the library. However, to begin with, books from the library must be taken to their doorsteps, which is not difficult as the library has a mobile unit. The librarian should set apart one day in a week to take the mobile unit to different parts of the town at specified hours to enable all those living in the vicinities to borrow and return the books.

6
Acquisition of Resources

Selection of resources, which include printed as well as electronic material, is the most important aspect of library administration, for the usefulness and popularity of the library depend primarily upon the resources it has. Unless the library has both printed and electronic resources to cater to the needs of the various sections of the community that it serves, the library will remain an unwanted institution. In other words, the library should have an adequate number of the right kind of books and other resources. There is no gainsaying the fact that selection of resources is not an easy task, as most novices in the profession tend to think. It is in fact, *the* most difficult one. The librarian of today knows that the computer, TV, VCR, CD, DVD, film projector, radio and such other electronic devices are absolutely inevitable in the library in order to not only attract but also effectively serve the clientele. Even when the library was concerned with printed material like books and periodicals alone, selection of resources had been one of the most difficult of the duties of a librarian. And now with these electronic devices taking the pride of place, resource selection has become a hundred-fold more difficult.

The first step in the process of resource selection is to have a clear-cut budget plan. It has been found that there is a tendency among some librarians not to buy enough books or other resource materials, even if suitable publications come out, in the early part of the financial year, hoping for better material to be brought out later in the year and to hold back as much of the funds as possible till the end of the financial year. This is a not a desirable policy to be followed. There is no certainty that better materials will be brought out later in the year; nor is there a guarantee that the suitable one(s) already in the market may not become out of stock by the end of the year. Finally at the end of the financial year, in order to preclude the budgetary allotment for books and other materials lapsing, they may be constrained to purchase substandard material and fill in the shelves with mediocre books and electronic resources. Some of them may be useless but they have been bought just to utilise the budget fully. This betrays a bankruptcy of policy and lack of proper planning.

Budgeting has to be meticulously planned if such predicaments are to be avoided but the plan need not be adhered to rigidly because lack of flexibility will create some other problem. So first and foremost, the librarian must apportion the funds for each subject, based on the total available budgetary outlay and the demand of the readers. Next, he should set apart a certain amount for purchasing books each month and that amount should not, as far as possible, be carried over for the subsequent month unless he is not able to find any useful books to be purchased that month. And if in a particular month he finds that many good publications have come out of the press, the total cost of which may exceed that month's budget, he should not hesitate to utilise the allocation earmarked for the following month or months to purchase those books. Consequently, sometimes at the end of the year he finds a few very good new publications, for which there is a great demand from the clientele and as such, need to be acquired urgently. But for purchasing those publications, there is no money in that year's budget. In such situations he need not get panicky; he may buy those books with the understanding that the bill would be paid only after the current financial year. He can rest assured that no vendor or publisher will refuse to supply the books on that account, for they are interested in sales and they know that the library has never been a defaulter and the amount will not remain a bad debt. Of course, as soon as the next year's allotment is released the pending bill or bills must be cleared promptly to retain the confidence of the vendor or publisher concerned, in the library. It is very important that the credibility of the library should not be lost.

The next step is apportioning the budgetary allotment among the various sections. It is preposterous to set apart, in the name of impartiality, equal amount for books in all subjects. There are two fundamental principles to be followed in selecting resource material for the library. These are mainly, utility and proportionality. These principles, however, are to be applied differently in different types of libraries. But whatever be the type of library, any deviation from these principles will inevitably lead to accumulation of useless material and ill-balanced collection resulting not only in the estrangement of readers but in the wastage of funds and shelf space as well.

First of all, the librarian should take care to ensure that books, which may not be of use do not come to the library shelves. So utility value is the most important aspect, not its cost or its format, that has to be taken into consideration when deciding to purchase a book. It may not be irrelevant here to recall a story, of doubtful authenticity though,[1] about Mahatma Gandhi. When young Mohandas first went to London to read Law, he used to be tempted to buy some of the articles displayed in shops. He would then question himself: "Is it absolutely necessary for me?" If the 'little voice' in him were to say "No", he would not buy that. This is how the resource materials for the library have to be selected. But the librarian has to decide not with reference to himself but to the users of the library. The usefulness of a book is relative and depends upon the category of members that the library has and the extension service that the library has undertaken. A book, which may be very useful in a school library, the members of which are primarily children, for example, would be absolutely useless in an adult public library or a special library and *vice-versa*. Similarly, the clientele of a public library in a rural area may not touch a book that is in great demand in the public library situated in a metropolitan city.

If, however, by mistake one or two useless books happen to be purchased, the librarian is sure to realise it in the course of a few months or even weeks when he finds that those volumes are not being borrowed by anyone. He has to be 'ruthless' in dealing with such books. He should not, then, hesitate to withdraw them at the end of the year, whatever might have been the cost of those books or howsoever good the condition of the books is. Nevertheless, they may be kept in the storage for another year to see if a demand for them would come and if that does not happen, discard them. But the librarian has to bear in mind that novels like those of Raja Rao and Saul Bellow for example, may not be taken out by readers as often as those of Kushwant Singh or Shobha De, although all of them are set in the modern period. Nevertheless, the librarian should not, on that account, refrain from buying such books or if purchased, withdraw them from the library. Works of Raja Rao and Saul Bellow are a heavier reading material than Kushwant Singh's and Shobha De's books and that is why they are taken out less often than the other two writers' books. Similarly, books of poems and even plays may not be of as much demand as those of fiction even in an adult public library or University library but still those works should not be withdrawn for that reason. Such books are a must in any library. So when thinking of withdrawing books of imaginative literature from the library, he should consider the literary value of the books, also.

The second principle, proportionality, demands that the library has a balanced collection of books. The wise librarian will purchase books on various subjects in proportion to the demand by the clientele. Demand, of course, would depend on the type of clientele. If the public library is serving a politically conscious community, the librarian will do well to purchase more of books on politics, trade unions, history, economics and allied disciplines. On the other hand, if the library is situated in a town where there are many schools and colleges, the librarian has to take into cognisance the needs of the academic section of the community and the library should have proportionately more books catering to their needs. Similarly, the librarians of children's libraries may find that books on religious and philosophical topics are not in demand at all – why, even in adult public libraries those subjects may not find many readers. There is, therefore, no need to buy many books on such subjects. Nevertheless, in an adult public library, there should be a representative collection of books on all subjects, for occasionally some reader or a casual visitor might want them. So proportionality implies that the library has books on all subjects but in proportion to the readers' demand.

The librarian is, thus, an appraiser in the sense that he has to evaluate a book or any instructional material that is to be purchased for the library. If it is a book, he estimates the value in terms of its usefulness, demand and cost before placing an order for it and on receipt assess the quality of its content and the format and only if he finds it satisfies the criteria mentioned above that he accessions it. But he cannot reject it on the basis of his judgement alone. In academic and special libraries for example, the book would have been suggested by one of the experts in the subject. But if the librarian thinks that it is not worth buying, he should take up the matter with the person who had suggested it and explain to him why, from the point of view of the library, it should not be acquired. However, if the expert thinks that it should be bought despite the drawbacks the librarian has pointed out, it may be accepted.

In formulating the acquisition policy of the library the following problem should not be lost sight of. What is the primary function of the library? In other words, the question is whether the library is an instrument of education or a means of recreation. Or, which of the two functions of the library has to be given more importance? This sounds rather pedantic and theoretical but in practical terms, this boils down to the question whether the library should have more books of informative literature or recreational reading material. To put it in simple terms, should the library have more of non-fiction or fiction? This is a problem that vexes many librarians and it may continue to do so forever. If the library is considered basically an educational tool, it should have predominantly non-fiction books but if it is looked upon primarily as a recreational centre (which only a commercial circulating library is) the collection should have more books of fiction than non-fiction.

Librarians, however, hold divergent views on this question, some strongly arguing that the primary responsibility of the library is 'to satisfy the demands of scholarship' while the others who vehemently oppose this view, aver that the library cannot ignore its duty to provide recreational reading material to its clientele. The former group want to see the library filled with serious reading material that would help readers intellectually enrich themselves and they think as an institution that is committed to the cause of education, it should not be a dumping ground for books of fiction. The latter group that favour having fiction in the collection, on the other hand, feel that fiction is not merely recreational stuff but is as much educative as non-fiction, the difference being that fiction educates indirectly unlike books of non-fiction, which educates directly. Fiction, they point out, gives the reader, whether a child or an adult, an insight into the character and psychology of human beings, men and women. Besides, books of fiction help him experience vicariously all that the characters in the story experience – love and hatred, indigence and affluence, pain and pleasure – why, everything that a human being in his real life goes through, for that matter. Most librarians, in fact, oppose the inclusion of fiction in the collection because they seem to think that fiction has no value whatsoever, the reason for which, perhaps, is that they identify fiction with only blockbusters and light romances. So reading fiction, they consider, is a waste of time. They do not realise that there are novels and short stories by writers like Nikos Kazantsaki (Greek), Sarat Chandra Chatterjee (Bengali), U.R.Anantha Murthy (Indo-Anglian), M. Mukundan (Malayalam), Mikhail Aleksandrovich Sholokhov (Russian), and a galaxy of dead and living novelists whose works are virtually penetrating critical studies of men and women and the society that forms the backdrop of their stories.

This problem, however, does not arise in the case of special libraries but is relevant to all other types of libraries. In the case of special libraries, the entire budget may have to be spent on books connected with the work being carried out by the institution that the library subserves because the prices of such books are usually very high, often exorbitant. So even if the institution would like to buy recreational books there will be little money left for it. However, it is desirable for special libraries also to have books meant for recreational reading on their shelves. A few books of imaginative literature may be added every year so that in course of time there will be an adequate collection of books to read for a change and help break the monotony of those who work in the parent institutions. These need not be novels and short stories alone. They may be essays, humorous, satirical and those written in a lighter vein, biographies, travelogues, collections of famous speeches, one-act plays, short poems and any such writings that help the reader relax mentally and more importantly, in the process widen his outlook.

It must, therefore, be accepted that, barring special libraries, all other types of libraries do play a dual role. The other two types of libraries – public libraries and academic libraries – are looked upon by the community and the circle of users as an educational tool as well as a recreational centre. And both these roles are of equal importance. Accepting that these libraries play a dual role, what should be the proportion of fiction to non-fiction? It is the public librarians and academic librarians that face this problem and not the special librarians as we have seen just now.

In the case of academic libraries, it may be possible to say that they are basically instruments of education than recreational centres. But it is exactly because those libraries are instruments of education that they are obliged to have fiction on their shelves. The course of study in literature of whatever language it is, has not only poems and plays but novels too and as such it is imperative that the college and university libraries have fiction in their collection. Public, both adult and juvenile as well as school libraries, however, should have more of fiction on their shelves than non-fiction. There is no doubt that public libraries are informal educational institutions but they are at the same time recreational centres too. Most public librarians would agree that a vast majority of the members of public libraries visit the library for recreational reading, for experience has shown that demand for books of fiction is undeniably much greater than that for non-fiction books. So if there are no books of fiction in the public library, not many users would care to step into the library and the membership is bound to dwindle.

As far as children's libraries, be it public or school, are concerned a good collection of fiction is imperative. This is necessary because surveys of reading interests of children have revealed that about 70 to 80 percent of the books that a child reads are fiction. (Mohanraj, 2004). Stories, it cannot be denied, have a positive role to play in the mental development of children. Besides, one of the educational aims of the school library is to inculcate reading habit in children and the best means for this is fiction. It has been observed that a child who reads of his own volition normally goes in for story books first and rarely, if at all, for a book of non-fiction. Of course, there could be a child or two who, seeing his parents or an adult at home reading a bulky tome, may pick up Jean-Paul Sartre's *Being and Nothingness* or some such book if not checked by the librarian. And, of course, return it without reading. A child who is a reluctant or a retarded reader and has to be coaxed to read will never take to reading if he or she is given a non-fiction book first even if it is an interesting one such as Gerald Durrel's *A Zoo in My Luggage* or a short and exciting life history like, for example, that of Subhas Chandra Bose, which is as gripping as a 'thriller'.

It is an irrefutable fact that children, once they master language and have acquired sufficient vocabulary to comprehend whatever the people around them say, ask for and listen with rapt attention to 'grandmother's tales'. So reading habit in a child could only be created through storybooks and not through non-fiction books, which are of no use for this purpose. Once the reading habit is created, the child, in due course, usually takes to reading non-fiction books, as he grows and develops new interests. An incident like a tsunami may kindle in the child an interest in a subject like earthquake and induce him to read books on it or he may take to reading books on extraterrestrial life and comets after reading a newspaper report on the sighting of an Unidentified Flying Object (UFO). Sometimes, his hobby or his favourite game could motivate him to read books on those subjects. Anyway, at least out of necessity, like class assignments or a project given by a teacher, he may be forced to read non-fiction books and this may gradually lead him on to the domain of informative books, possibly never to return to imaginative literature. So public and academic libraries should have the right mix of fiction and non-fiction books – more of the former than the latter – on their shelves.

Who is the authority to decide what is to be purchased? Public libraries are controlled either by the Local Self-Government or the State Government and in a few exclusive libraries, which do not depend on government grant, the management is vested in a Committee elected by the members. The Local Self-Government or the State Government in the case of public libraries or the Managing Committee in the case of private libraries that holds the purse strings is, naturally, the ultimate authority and they select books for the library. The librarian may have absolutely no voice in the selection of resources. Ideally, however, the government department controlling the public library may choose books for a certain percentage of the budgetary outlay and the librarian should be free to select books for the remaining amount, for it is he who knows the local requirements. The same procedure should apply to unaided exclusive libraries too; the members of the Managing Committee of the private library may choose books for a certain percentage of the budgetary allotment, giving the librarian who alone knows the requirements of the readers, the liberty to buy whatever books he thinks are necessary. It has been found from experience that most members of Managing Committees of exclusive libraries buy books without reference to the needs of the clientele. They invariably select books haphazardly and mainly on subjects, which they are interested in, resulting in a lop-sided development of the library. Moreover, most government officials connected with the public library and members of the Managing Committees of exclusive libraries may not be aware of the latest publications as much as the librarian; nor would they have any knowledge of publishers' lists, bibliographies and other sources to choose books from.

There are certain publications like general encyclopaedias, year-books, dictionaries and such other reference books that would be of use in any library, whether located in an urban or rural area. Similarly, works of imaginative literature and even some factual books like biographies, for example, would be relevant to libraries serving any community, irrespective of the class of people it is composed of. Such books may be purchased by the controlling authority and distributed to all public libraries. But as far as books on other subjects are concerned, the needs of each community differ and the librarian of each library is the best judge to decide what books and other resources are to be purchased for the library over which he presides.

The public librarian, if he is authorised to select resource materials for the library, should not keep himself confined to the library. He has to be in constant touch with the users, discuss the books with them and try to fathom their interests and tastes. But in order to do this the librarian himself should have read the books in the library. This, of course, is an impossible task today for any individual, howsoever avid a reader he is, when the world of knowledge is expanding at an incredible rate and books on all subjects are flowing out of the press in hundreds almost everyday. But he can, no doubt, read the blurbs of books or the reviews that appear in various periodicals. And he should necessarily skim through certain books that are popular among the clientele to know the reading trend of the community. Apart from this, it is imperative that the public librarian periodically conducts reading surveys in the community that the library serves and maintains records of those surveys.

This is necessary because the interests and tastes of the reading public are always in a flux; the authors or the subjects that are popular at a given time may not find any place in the subsequent survey. Hence the librarian has to modify the acquisition policy on the basis of the findings of his survey. This will enable him to select the right kind of books as well as to avoid being accused of prejudice in the selection.

Besides, he should welcome suggestions by the users. It is true that in a democratic society like ours individual freedom is a fundamental right. However, this does not mean that if a reader suggests a seditious or a pornographic book invoking his constitutional right, it must be acquired. Saying that he has the right to use the road, no one can saunter along the middle of the road at peak hour and cause traffic jam. Nevertheless, the librarian should not arbitrarily reject a book suggested by a reader but gently and tactfully explain to him and try to convince him why it cannot be accepted for the library. If he stubbornly refuses to be convinced, do not argue but do not buy. Anyway, it is always desirable to place orders for books "On Approval" basis so that the librarian reserves the right to reject a book if found unsuitable on examination.

The procedure for selection of resources in academic libraries, however, is different. In all these types of libraries, be it school, college or university, as far as reference and general books are concerned, the librarian may use his discretion and buy books. But as far as books pertaining to various disciplines are concerned, the librarian cannot and should not unilaterally take decisions. He has to take the advice of the members of the teaching staff, each of whom is an expert in the subject that he or she handles. Naturally, he is familiar with the literature of his subject and knows the books that the department concerned needs. The librarian, should, however, help the teachers by supplying the latest catalogues and publishers' lists for them to select from and suggesting books that he thinks would be of use in the library. The same procedure holds good for special libraries too. In the case of Bar Council or High Court libraries, the members of the Bar and the Bench are the right judges and in libraries of research institutions, the research scholars are the ultimate authority in the selection of resources. Not that the librarian has no voice – judging by the demands from the users, he would have known the weakness in the collection and to fill in those lacunae, he could either suggest some books to the Heads of Departments concerned or ask them to suggest books to make good the deficiency.

The modern library, whether it is public, academic or special, is not a repository of printed documents only. It should necessarily have various other instructional and informative materials like films, filmstrips, audio/video cassettes, CDs and DVDs. Possibly, coming years may witness many other new electronic instructional materials. Be that as it may, today the librarian faces the problem of choosing the electronic materials mentioned above. Although the policy and principles of selection are the same, selection of these electronic resources are more difficult than selecting books. Being audio-visual materials the effect of these on the minds of viewers is far more than that of printed materials.

No one would have forgotten the hue and cry raised against the celluloid version of Kazantsaki's *The Last Temptation of Christ*, when it was screened but the book on which the film was based had been in circulation for quite some time before that, without even causing a whimper in protest. The reason for it is, as stated above, the impact that an audio-visual media will have on the human mind because what is described in print is brought vividly before the eyes of the viewer in a motion picture. When he read the book, he would not have visualised the scene, that he found outrageous in the film, so graphically as when it was viewed on the silver screen. And so the librarian has to be doubly careful in selecting films or any visual electronic materials. As in the case of a work of imaginative literature, the aesthetic value of the film or cassette or disc should not be sacrificed under any circumstance. However, films like *Lady Chatterly's Lover,* the one based on Lawrence's novel of the same name, or *The Last Temptation of Christ* because of the literary value of the novels on which it is based, would be desirable additions, for they are audio-visual presentation of classics. It is better to avoid acquiring a film like *The Bandit Queen* – even the video copy of that movie. But in case the library acquires movies like the ones mentioned above, they should be screened to adult audiences only. Apart from providing aesthetic experience, the audio-visual resources should help stimulate viewers' imagination and widen their knowledge.

Before acquiring a film or a video cassette/CD/DVD, the librarian should have a preview of the material to make sure that the picture is clear and there is no audio distortion. If it is for juvenile library, there should not be blatantly lewd scenes and the dialogue should be free from too much colloquialism and vulgarisms. Seldom do we find films devoid of violence these days as we are living in a world of violence and terrorism and naturally, this will be reflected in films (and books too). As Lewis, in his paper on *Three Ways of Writing for Children,* points out, even children should not be denied "the knowledge that they are born into a world of death, violence, wounds, adventure, heroism and cowardice, good and evil". But films that glorify or condone violence and terrorism are not desirable. On the other hand, movies like *Kalapani,* which depicts an episode in the saga of our struggle for independence and one like *Bombay* that has a message, which is relevant at all times must be acquired. These movies can be recommended even for the children's library, the violence and bloodshed in them notwithstanding, for the children should know how much the partisan forces of our freedom movement suffered and also be conscious of the oneness of mankind. Movies that preach hatred of a particular religious group or a community and encourage sectarianism must not be purchased under any circumstance, either for the adult library or children's library.

In evaluating the resource material to be purchased for the library, the one essential quality required for a librarian to be able to choose the right material is extensive reading and wide interest. These two – extensive reading and wide interest – should, however, go hand in hand with open-mindedness, which implies absence of national, political, linguistic, religious, caste or any kind of prejudice. If the librarian is interested in political science, history, archaeology, anthropology and such other allied subjects, he should not refrain from – or allot proportionately small amount for – buying books on other disciplines than in the subjects in which he is interested. Similarly, he should not keep buying only art films and abjure feature films altogether, for there are many feature films with messages. In other words, his personal bias should not come into play when he selects resources for the library – the touchstone should be the readers and the community alone.

But under no circumstance should he sacrifice quality to please the clientele or even to attract more members to the library. This does not mean that the library has to be stuffed with serious books and 'high-brow' art films only, for it should not be forgotten that the library is a centre for research as well as recreation, for education and entertainment. Even a scholarly person and an art film enthusiast would at times go in for recreational reading or may like to watch popular comedies and a reader of light material may occasionally decide to go in for serious stuff. So along with modern erudite and old classical works of non-fiction and fiction, there can be a sprinkling of light reading material. Similarly, there should be a judicious mixture of documentary films and popular but clean feature films. However, extra care must be taken in selecting those books and films/video cassettes, particularly blockbusters and feature films. In short, the librarian should appraise *objectively*, whatever material is being purchased for the library.

Footnotes

1 This is not found in his autobiography, *The Story of My Experiments with Truth* but the writer had only heard this repeatedly said by many when he was a child and does not know the source of the story.

7
Classification

Library science is the study or the principles and practices of library care and management and a person who has specialised in it, is the librarian. He would, thus, be a specialist in library techniques like classification and cataloguing, without at least a basic knowledge of which, care and administration of the library is not possible. In fact, long back scholars and librarians had recognised the need for and the importance of both classification and cataloguing in providing effective library services. A professional librarian should, therefore, have a good grasp of the technique of classification and cataloguing. Since classification of books precedes the work of cataloguing, for no book is usually catalogued without first being classified, it would be appropriate to discuss the technique of classification before going into the theory and technique of cataloguing, which shall be dealt with in the next chapter.

What is classification? Classification, in general, is the process of systematically grouping objects on the basis of certain of their characteristics that are common to them and separating those that do not have these characteristics. The lower animals identify herbs, fruits and roots that can be eaten and those that cannot be eaten – this, no doubt, is an act of classification. These animals, including the anthropoid primates like the chimpanzee, orang-utan and gorilla belonging to the family of *Pongidae*, however, unlike the *Homo sapiens* classify edible and non-edible things instinctively, and certainly not intelligently. In any case, they do not classify as we human beings do by taking into consideration characteristics that are common to a particular group of things.

Millions of years must have elapsed before the *Pongidae's* forelegs got transformed into hands and they stepped out of the knuckle-walking gait to attain erect posture and bipedal gait, giving rise to the first man, *Homo erectus* of the Pleistocene epoch, considered one of the direct ancestors of modern man, the *Homo sapiens.* Being on a step higher than *Pongidae,* the brain of *Homo erectus* could not have been very different from but was certainly much more developed than that of a *Pongidae.* Wallace, the celebrated biologist, says, the brain of even the savage was more developed and complex than that of any other animal, including anthropoids. (Wallace, 1870). Hence, the level of intelligence of even the Man of the period of the Lower Status of Savagery would naturally have been higher than that of the other animals, including those of the *Pongidae* family.

It is the gait and hands that helped man wage a constant war against Nature, thus providing the basis for the gradual development of articulate speech and the brain (Engels, 1974) of which mind, with its concomitants of intelligence and emotions, is the product. Morgan, the well-known anthropologist, points out that the commencement of articulate speech belongs to this period- the period of savagery (Morgan, 1978). All these biological changes made him different from other animals – he became an intelligent animal and unlike all the other animals he was not guided by instinct. And so he must have classified edible and non-edible things not instinctively but intelligently. He might have seen his fellow beings or other animals dying or taking ill after eating a fruit, which, though looking attractive, was poisonous. This experience would have made him avoid that and the knowledge gained from this experience must have been passed on from individual to individual by word of mouth. Eventually, he began to classify the objects around him by recognising the special features of each object. And ever since man has been classifying objects intelligently.

Man, as stated above, using his newly acquired faculties, the brain and hands, has been locked in a perpetual struggle against Nature in order to harness the forces of nature to make his life more comfortable. That in turn helped the further development of his brain and his skill in using his hands and day by day, so to speak, he became more and more adroit and more and more dextrous. Apart from this, in the course of this incessant conflict with nature he had to overcome many hurdles for which he had to think and as a result, he accumulated a large amount of knowledge. Initially the knowledge that he had gained was a conglomeration of ideas and as his brain developed further he began to classify systematically into groups and sub-groups. In other words, he began to classify knowledge and over the years, he applied this technique to various objects that he saw around him.

Thus, he classified all animals and plants including human beings into two groups, male and female. In ancient India the Indo-Aryans classified human beings into three groups, medically and philosophically and into four groups, socially. The Ayurvedic physicians classified them as (i) *vaata* (gas) type, (ii) *pitha* (bile) type and (iii) *kapha* (Phlegm) type, while the Sankhya philosophers divided them into *saatviks*, *raajasviks* and *taamasviks*. The former classification was based on the physical make-up of human beings, while the latter on the basis of the character or mental attitudes of human beings. Socially, the early Indo-Aryans classified human beings into four classes or *varnas*, as Brahmana, Kshatriya, Vysia and Sudra on the basis of their vocations and in later years these four groups were further sub-divided into castes or *jatis*, again based on the vocation or trade of each group. In modern times, Karl Marx classified human beings into two economic classes, the nomenclatures of classes changing in consonance with the changes taking place in the economic structure of society. In the slave society, for example, they were classified as slaves and masters, which in the feudal society became serfs and landlords and in the succeeding capitalist society, the proletariat and the bourgeoisie.

In fact, classification is done in all spheres of human activity. In a supermarket, for example, we find one section dealing with grocery, another section with medicines, a third with garments, a fourth with leather goods and so on. In each of these sections, the traders keep their wares classified depending on how the customers would demand the articles. For example, garments may be classified first as men's clothes and women's attire and again by brands, cost or by any other criteria by which the customers normally ask for them. Obviously, therefore, the criterion they apply for classifying the commodities on sale is 'demand'. Hence, classification of anything, in general, is always based on some criterion, which distinguishes one set from the others.

A library in which the books are shelved without being classified is only a dumping ground of books but not a library howsoever big and valuable the collection may be. It is like some of those second hand bookshops that are found in certain towns and cities, in which some books can be seen piled up in a corner, some tied up in bundles and heaped in another corner and a few of them strewn all over the floor. When a customer goes and asks for any particular book, the shopkeeper may not know if he has such a book. In order to find out if that book is available there or not the customer with the help of the shopkeeper may have to spend hours together wading through those piles and bundles. The book would have been there but yet they might fail to lay their hands on it. So if books in a library are not classified the patron who comes looking for any particular book may have to go back disappointed, the position of the librarian being no different from that of the shopkeeper described above.

Several criteria can be adopted for classifying the collection of books in a library. It can be done alphabetically by their titles or authors' names; it can be grouped by their sizes; it can be separated by the year of publication. The publisher too can be a criterion and the books of different publishers can be put together in separate groups. But the books in a library are not for display; they are meant for use. So just as in a supermarket, 'demand' is to be the basic criterion in the library too. In other words, books have to be classified keeping in view the mode of demand of users and from experience, it had been found that users always looked for books by subjects. No one ever asks for a book published in a particular year or by a particular publisher; nor does anyone ask for a folio or quarto. The readers invariably ask for books of a certain subject or those written by an author they like. They may also ask if the library has a book with a certain title.

In order, therefore, to facilitate the use of the books in the library, or to put it differently, to satisfy the first four Laws of Library Science enunciated by S.R.Ranganathan, (Ranganathan, 1931) it is imperative that books in a library are properly classified. And library, as the fifth Law (Ranganathan, 1931) states, being "a growing organisation" the librarian should not attempt to classify, as he likes, because at some stage or other, it is bound to break down. Some local classification systems designed to meet local demands, like for example, the Cheltenham Classification, however, seemed to have worked well, creating no problems. This system, described in The Cheltenham Classification by E. S. Fegan and M. Cant, was conceived and devised at Cheltenham Ladies' College, UK. (Ralph, 1960). The subjects, in this system, have been divided keeping in mind the school curriculum of the region and must have worked successfully there for some years but it is doubtful if it had worked for very long and certainly it may not be applicable anywhere else. It is desirable that the books are classified according to one of the internationally accepted systems of classification. All these systems of classification had been devised logically, after giving considerable thought to the needs of the user as well as to the intrinsic connection between the various subjects and based on the long and rich experience of the respective classificationists.

Broadly speaking, book classification is the application of knowledge classification to the world of books. It may not be wrong to say that Aristotle's (384-322 BC) general classification of knowledge and to some extent, the ideas of Marcus Terrentius Varro (116-27 BC), the great Roman scholar and 'a satirist of stature' who was Julius Caesar's librarian paved the way for book classification. A person, who is interested in or researching on band spectrum, for example, may require books on various aspects of Spectroscopy or dispersion of light like for example, the technique of spectrum, line spectrum, hyperfine structure apart from other topics pertaining to light. He may also need books on Raman effect, Kerr effect and such other special effects in addition to books on other allied topics, like infrared spectroscopy, ultraviolet spectroscopy for collateral reading. And possibly, he would look for books on specific applications of spectroscopy. So the classification system should bring, as far as possible, books on all these topics in adjacent shelves. Besides, he may have to refer to certain books in the class Mathematics as well as Science in general. And depending on what specific problem of band spectrum he is investigating, he may have to reach out to several shelves with books on other related disciplines, apart from the shelf containing books on Physics, of which the subject of his investigation is directly connected. The requirements of library users, therefore, demand arranging of books in such a way that books of the same subjects are put together and those of the interconnected or related subjects are kept juxtaposed on the shelves. Any good scheme of classification cannot but meet this natural requirement of the user and this is an important feature of a good scheme of classification.

In general terms, the most important characteristic of a good classification system is that it is designed logically, taking into cognisance the correlation between different subjects and the subdivisions of each subject. The other necessary characteristics of a good classification inevitably flow from this. The classification has to be comprehensive, encompassing the entire field of human knowledge, lest the user may not be able to get what he wants. Howsoever comprehensive the scheme is, it will fail to satisfy the patron unless each subject is fully analysed and all its subdivisions are also worked out in detail. Besides, the scheme of classification should have flexibility, which means the properties of expandability and adaptability. So an ideal classification scheme is one that is not rigid and can be expanded and adapted to meet local requirements by making necessary additions to and/or deletions of certain subdivisions in the schedules of classification.

That the Dewey Decimal Classification system has these qualities cannot be denied and as such is, undoubtedly, an excellent system of classification. But it is not totally free from defects, the chief drawback being that it is centred very much on the US and West Europe. This defect, however, is obviated by its flexibility, for although US/West European centred, it can be easily adapted to meet the requirements of Asia, Africa and any other region. The Canon of Local Variations does not operate so well in the case of Colon Classification Scheme. Two other points in favour of the Dewey Decimal system is that it is revised and expanded periodically to accommodate new disciplines that spring up subsequent to the publication of one edition and authoritative abridged editions of the system for use in small and children's libraries are also available.

Being US / West European oriented, the Dewey System cannot be used as it is, in the libraries of India or of any Asian or African country and even of East European countries. For example, if you take a look at the Class '800 Literature' you will find that literature of America (US) and West European languages are allotted class numbers but literature of all other languages are clubbed under the class number 890. Again, in the Class '200 Religion', Christianity alone has been dealt with in detail while all other religions are dumped together under one class number, 290. The librarian who adopts this scheme of classification in India may confront such problems in some other classes also. Nevertheless, this is the best classification system that can be used in Indian libraries, the redeeming feature in the case of this system of Classification being that variations and deviations are permitted and this is possible too. However, care must be taken not to disturb the basic structure of the scheme. These deviations must be noted in the margin at the appropriate places in the Tables so that uniformity can be maintained. There is an abridged version of the system that can be used in high school libraries and juvenile public libraries. A still more shortened version of this system, adapted by the School Library Association Dewey Sub-committee for British schools, which can be used in elementary school libraries, is also available. Although this is compiled for British schools, with a few modifications it can be used in Indian schools too.

Of course, no scheme of classification is flawless. As Melvil Dewey, the father of Decimal Classification, himself puts it, "a scheme can be satisfactory in use only to those who realise... inherent difficulties and are satisfied because of their knowledge that a plan free from annoying difficulties is wholly unattainable." (Dewey, 1951) So the librarian cannot hope to find a perfect scheme of classification. He has only to be judicious in choosing a system of classification for the library and no consideration other than the library and its constituency should play a part in making the choice.

There are nine well-known systems of classification, which are:

a) **Decimal Classification.** This system was devised by Melvil Dewey (1837-1903), an American librarian. On graduating at Amherst College, Massachusettes, in 1874, Dewey joined as Assistant Librarian at that institution itself and two years later, in 1876, he published *A Classification and Subject Index for Cataloguing and Arranging the Books and Pamphlets of a Library*. Popularly known today as the *Dewey Decimal Classification*, this system is now the most widely used in the US, the UK, Canada and several countries of Latin America, Europe, Asia, Africa and Australia – in all, not less than ninety countries including India – and has been translated in about twelve languages. It is the most user friendly of all the systems of classification and that perhaps is the secret of its popularity. Its greatest advantage is that it is updated periodically by a team of experts.

b) **Expansive Classification.** Devised by Charles Ammi Cutter (1837-1903), an American librarian, this is called 'expansive' because Cutter seems to have "compiled seven successive classification schemes, each an expansion of the one before." (Hawkins, 1061). This scheme, published in 1891, has been described by J.D.Brown (1862-1914), the distinguished British librarian, as "one of the most scientific and complete schemes of classification."

c) **Library of Congress Classification.** This system is not devised by any individual but is the outcome of the co-operative efforts of many librarians and subject specialists. It came into being when Herbert Putnam, the librarian of the Library of Congress, along with his staff decided to reclassify the books in the library in the early twentieth century. They rejected the Dewey Decimal system and preferred an arrangement "based on the order devised" by Cutter. The greatest advantage of this system is that its schedules are regularly revised and updated.

d) **Universal Decimal Classification**. Sponsored by Federation Internationale de Documentation, this system, which saw the light of day in 1905, was devised by Paul-Marie-Ghislain Paul in collaboration with Henri-Marie Lafontaine, both of whom, interestingly, were lawyers and bibliophiles. Although based on Dewey's Decimal System of Classification, they employ various symbols other than Arabic numerals for its notation. This system is said to have grown out of the international subject index of the Institute Internationale du Bibliographie et Brussels; hence it is also called Brussels Classification. "It is based on the principle of processing from the general to the more particular so that related concepts are brought together in a more helpful way than can be achieved by alphabetical or other arrangements." (Lloyd, 1965). This is the system used in the United Nations Library apart from many European and Asian libraries.

e) **Subject Classification**. This has been devised by James Duff Brown (1862-1914), a British librarian, based on the concept that matter, life, mind and record are the four facets of human knowledge. Its notation, unlike that of Dewey Decimal Classification is mixed but is not too complex to comprehend. This is used in many libraries in the UK. It has been opined (Howard, 1955) that Brown's arrangement of main classes is an improvement on Dewey and that with certain modifications, this system would be very effective in small and medium-sized libraries.

f) **Colon Classification.** Devised by S.R.Ranganathan (1892- 1972), an eminent Indian librarian, and published in 1933, this system is used in several research, University, college and public libraries in India. The fundamental difference between this system and other systems is that while all others are enumerative classifications, this is an Analytico-Synthetic classification. As such, this classification analyses the different facets of a subject and synthesises them with the help of various connecting symbols based on certain rules, canons, laws and principles. The notation like that of the Subject Classification is mixed and includes all letters of the English alphabet (both capitals and small letters), some letters of the Greek alphabet, Arabic numerals and all punctuation marks. Several editions of the schedules of this system had come out during the lifetime of Ranganathan. But since his death, this seems to have been stymied with the result the schedules do not reflect the many new developments in the field of knowledge.

g) **Bibliographic Classification.** This system, which was devised by Henry Evelyin Bliss, was first published in 1935, to be followed by a comprehensive edition in 1940-'53. It divides knowledge into thirty-five main classes and is, as its name indicates, primarily a bibliographic tool, useful particularly for classifying special subject fields. The notation, like the Colon or Subject Classification, is mixed, comprising all the twenty-six letters of the English alphabet, both upper and lower cases, and the nine digits of the Arabic numerals apart from the punctuation marks, the coma and the apostrophe. These two punctuation marks are used for separating adjacent letters or groups of them. Unlike in other systems of classification, this is characterised by an abundance of cross-references.

h) **Soviet Library Classification.** Published in 1959, it is not attributed to any individual, as is the case with several other systems of classification; its authorship lies with the Library Commission of the Academy of Science of the erstwhile Soviet Union. Its approach to classification is totally different from that of the other systems. As is evident from its structure, it is devised from the point of view of Marxism-Leninism and as such, the scientific laws governing Nature, Society and Knowledge constitute the three pillars on which this system is built. All other classes are arranged on the basis of the historical developments caused by the dialectical relationship between Nature and Society.

i) **Chinese Classification.** This is very different from the systems of classification devised by Western classificationists or Ranganathan but in a way similar to that of the Soviet System. Knowledge is classified based on the principles of Marxist philosophy, and the scheme "has an enumerative structure and may be distinguished by its detail of analysis of and dependence on the corpus of Marxist literature".

The various systems of classification described above may not be adequate enough to meet the requirements of libraries stocking books exclusively on specialised fields of knowledge. Those libraries, therefore, develop their own systems of classification so that they can categorise books on the subject to a much deeper degree of specificity. The most well-known of such specialised systems is that of the National Library of Medicine in the US. This system, which is based on the Library of Congress Classification, has been adopted by many other major medical libraries in that country.

The problem for the librarian lies in choosing the system appropriate to the library over which he presides.

Needless to say, it is not desirable for a library, howsoever small, to use a locally improvised system. The most commonly adopted device is to allot the first letter of the term by which the subject is known, like for example, M for Mathematics or F for Fiction followed by the initial letter of the surname of the author to individualise the books. Of course, no trained librarian would do this because he knows that such a system is bound to break down as the library grows and more and more books are added in each subject. There could be more than one subject the names of which begin with the same letter, like for example, Geology and Geography or Philosophy and Psychology or Mathematics and Medicine. And when each subject is further divided, the result would be nothing short of utter chaos.

So, conscious of this and such other problems, even if the library is very small consisting of a few hundred books only, no professional librarian would try out his hand at devising his own system of classification and classifying those books. He knows the library will not remain small for ever. "Library is a growing organism" and a librarian always prefers to adopt an internationally accepted system of classification, with which he knows that he will not confront any difficulties like that. The type of service expected of the library and the community that the library serves constitute the touchstone by which he decides the system to be adopted. It is preposterous, for example, to adopt the Bibliographic Classification System or even, the Colon Classification System in a small rural public library. The most suitable system in such libraries, is the Dewey Decimal Classification, which is easy for a layman to follow and for an untrained library assistant or attendant to replace books in the shelves. On the other hand for a research library, Colon Classification or Universal Decimal Classification may be preferred because with those systems, it is possible to classify books to much greater depth than with Dewey Decimal

Classification or Subject Classification.

Once the system of classification to be adopted is decided upon, the classifier faces the difficult task of classifying the books. The first step in classifying a book is to determine what the book is about. It is true that in many cases this may be clear from the titles, for the title usually indicates the subject of a book. So it is not difficult to classify every book. A book of poems, like for example *An Anthology of Poems* or *The Columbia-Viking Desk Encyclopaedia*, is not problematic, for the titles tell you in which classes the books are to be placed. Similarly, a book like *The Observer's Book of Sculpture* by William Gaunt or one like *Marx for Beginners*, tr. by Richard Appignanesi, can easily be classified.

On the other hand, classifying the book, *Cows, Pigs, Wars and Witches* by Marvin Harris is not as easy as all the above mentioned books. In the case of those four books mentioned above, the subject matter is evident from their titles, but it is not so in the case of a book like that of Marvin Harris's. The classifier should not take for granted that the book deals with the zoology of the cow and the pig just because the title contains those words; the word 'war' in the title should not mislead him to presume that it is a book of history and the word 'witches' should not be taken to conclude that the book is on black magic. The book does not deal with zoology, war or black magic; it deals entirely with a different subject. So the title of the book does not reveal the subject. We shall presently see what would give a clue about the content of this book.

In certain cases, while the title may be misleading, from the name of the author the classifier can determine the content of the book and the class to which the book belongs. The books, *Crime and Punishment* and *The Good Earth*, for example, are of that kind. There could be no librarian who has not heard of or does not know the field in which Feodor Mikhaliovich Dostoyevsky and Pearl S. Buck have distinguished themselves and if there is one, he or she is unfit to be a librarian. So when the librarian sees the names of the authors of these books he can classify the books under Russian and English Fiction respectively and not under Law/ Sociology and Geology/Geography/Ecology respectively as their titles seem to indicate. But there are cases in which even the authors' names would take the librarian on the wrong track. *The Rule of the Monk* by Giueseppe Garibaldi[1] and *The Insider* by P.V.Narasimha Rao are two examples of such books. Looking at the names of authors the librarian may give the class number of "Politics" or "History" for these books, as the authors are well-known political personalities who fought (in different ways, though) for the freedom of their respective countries. Both these books have autobiographical elements in them but they are not autobiographies either; they cannot be put in any class other than fiction, Italian and English respectively. The classifier cannot, therefore, depend solely on the title or the author of a book to determine its class number.

So let us see, when the subject matter of the book is not clear from its title, what else will indicate the subject matter? The Table of Contents, to a great extent, can be relied upon to find out the subject and in case this also fails to reveal the subject, the librarian must go through the Preface or the blurb. If from those too, the subject is not apparent, the librarian may have to glance through the book or even read it thoroughly. Sometimes, the librarian may find it difficult to decide even after an examination of the book, in which case he has to seek the advice of the subject specialist. Occasionally, even if the librarian is able to decide upon the main class, the help of a subject specialist may be required to determine the division, section and sub-section to which the book could be assigned. Anyway, as far as the book, *Cows, Pigs, Wars and Witches* is concerned, if the classifier reads the blurb, he can confidently classify the book under 'Anthropology'.

Many books have fanciful titles like *The Fall of a Sparrow* and *Wings of Fire* – going solely by these titles, no librarian would assign the class number of 'Biography' to these books. There are also books with titles that are not fanciful at all but misleading. For example, a book entitled *Masonry* could be one on the trade of the brickworker, i.e., the mason, or on freemasonry, the principles and practices of a world wide secret society founded in the 1330s. The term 'masonry' is used for both but the two, as you know, are totally different subjects and it will be ridiculous if the classifier, judging by the title, blindly gives the class number 690, presuming that it is a treatise on bricklaying, while the book is actually on freemasonry, the class number of which is 336.1! So it is always desirable that the librarian does not depend on the title alone or the name of the author for deciding on the class number of a book, even if the subject matter of the book is apparent from it.

After the subject of the book has been determined, the classifier has to decide the proper place in the schedules to which the book could be assigned. The classifier should not be a stickler for the rules laid down in the particular System of Classification that is used in the library. As stated in an earlier chapter, the library today is essentially reader centric and so the classifier has to bear in mind the clientele of the library. He has to think of the objectives of the library, on the basis of which, decide on the class to which the book may be assigned. In other words, the classifier decides on the class number according to a rule of thumb. That alone will bring the book to the notice of the readers, especially of those for whom the book would be of most use. On the other hand, if the book is classified strictly as per the rules, it could sometimes be as good as lost. It is only an experienced classifier who is keenly aware of the aims of the library as well as the requirements of the category of users can decide if a book like, *The Gulag Archipelago* by Solzhenitsyn should be classified under 'Crime' or along with the history of the country, on which the subject of the book has a direct bearing. Even if he decides to put it under 'Crime', he has to choose between, 343 (Criminal Law) and 364.13 (Crimes and Offences against the State).

It is, of course, easy to classify a book like *A Brief Survey of Indian History* by K.M.Panikkar or *India After Independence* by Bipan Chandra, et al but not one like *Viceroys of India* by M. Bence-Jones and *The White Mughal* by William Dalrymple. No classifier can make a mistake in assigning numbers for the first two but the other two may be, to some extent, problematic. The classifier has to decide where those books will be useful – in Indian History section or Biography section. If those books are classified under 954.03 'Indian History – British rule', it is imperative that cross references must be given in the catalogue under 'Biography' because a reader looking in the catalogue for the biography of any particular Viceroy for example, may miss this book altogether if the cross reference is not given. Similarly, if it is classified under 'Biography', cross-references must be given in the history section of the catalogue. This is necessary because, a reader who may be looking for the biography of a particular Viceroy, thinking that there could be some book on him in the library, without knowing either the author or the exact title of this or any book, may search the subject index (under 'Indian History') only, after failing to find the book in the 'Biography' shelf.

After the subject matter of the book has been determined, the classifier has to assign the classification number, which is not as simple as it seems because it cannot be classified blindly, taking into account the content of the book. What is more crucial is not the subject matter of the book, but the reader, for the number that is assigned has to be the one that will bring the book to the notice of the reader. There are several numbers that can be assigned for a book on fish, like for example, 574.92074, 597, 639, 799 or any other depending on the specific aspect dealt with in the book. If it is a book on fishing as a sport, the appropriate number for the book is certainly not 597 or any of its sub-divisions but any number from 799.1 to 799.17. However, fishing as an industry has to be classified in 639.2 or its subdivisions as the case may be but a book dealing with the manufacture of fishing equipments has to be classed under 688.79. The economic aspect of fishing may have to go to the class 338.3 and the laws pertaining to fishing will be 799.026.

All this has been pointed out only to emphasise the heavy responsibility that the classifier has. A book erroneously classified and consequently wrongly catalogued and placed among the books not even remotely connected with the subject matter of the book in question, is as good as a lost book. Let alone the readers, even the reference librarian will not be able to lay his hands on it, when required. So it is always desirable to read the blurb or even skim through before finally deciding on the call number to be given.

Footnotes

1 This book is out of print now. However, this has been taken as an example because it is similar to Narasimha Rao's in many respects – a novel with autobiographical elements in it, written by a patriot who fought (with arms, though, unlike Narasimha Rao) for the freedom of his country.

8
Cataloguing

The library may have all the books in the world, with sufficient funds at its disposal to procure whatever book is being published in any part of the world and a spacious, well-ventilated, functionally efficient, architecturally elegant building provided with rows and rows of bookcases to house this collection, managed by a team of professionally qualified librarians. How does a reader who comes to the library find the book or the information that he wants? Whoever enters the library having such a large collection of books may possibly wander among the rows and rows of bookcases, not knowing where the book that he wants is. He may spend hours and hours, perhaps days and days, in the library searching for the book and still may fail to find it, unless he stumbles on it. Even the librarians, who have processed and shelved those books, depending on their memory may not be able to lay their hands on the desired material, particularly if the collection is very large. In fact, the library is not worth its name and the librarian is not worth his salt, if the user is not able to get the book or the information that he wants at the right time in the shortest time possible. If the reader does not get the book he wants, whether it is for recreational reading or research the very purpose of the library is defeated.

The catalogue is the tool that helps locate a book on the shelf or retrieve any information from the books that are in the library. It is an essential tool that indicates where a particular book is in the shelf; it is also an index that points to the book(s) containing the information that is being sought. It will also tell the reader what all books are there in the library by the author or on the subject he is interested in. If there is no catalogue, all the money spent on procuring and stacking a huge collection and paying the library staff to take care of the institution is a sheer waste of public funds because those who come to the library to read a book or collect some information from a certain book may have to go back disappointed. In short, a library cannot function effectively without a catalogue and so no library, howsoever small it is, can neglect the work of cataloguing its collection.

It may not be wrong to say that the foundation for cataloguing was laid by Callimachus, the Greek poet and critic, who flourished in the 3rd century BC. The first library catalogue, as far as we know, was made by him when he was the librarian of the Library of Alexandria, to which post he was appointed by Ptolemy II Philadelphus of Egypt. The most famous of his prose writings, was a detailed and critical biographical catalogue of the authors of the works that were in the Alexandrian library. He had given it the title, *Pinakes*, meaning 'Tablets'. It is intriguing why he had given that title for his work because the library of Alexandria held papyrus and vellum scrolls and not clay tablets. In almost every library of the ancient world, there seems to have been some kind of list of its holdings, examples of a few of which can be seen in various museums.[1]

Let us see what a catalogue, as we understand by the term today, is. A catalogue is a list but 'list' is the general term used to indicate series of names, figures or words, like for example a list of the people. This may be in any order – alphabetical order of their names, sex-wise or age-wise depending on the purpose for which it is prepared. An inventory too is a list but it is a complete and detailed list of articles, that are in stock in a store for instance, and tells how many of each item there are, and what they are worth. In the context of a library, the inventory is a comprehensive list of not just the books but all types of articles like pieces of furniture that constitute the movable property of the library. An inventory is maintained for the purpose of taking stock of all the holdings at the end of every financial year. Catalogues of books, which booksellers or publishers bring out are intended to help market the books that are on sale. These catalogues invariably give brief notes on the content of the book and the *curriculum vitae* of the author – mostly a condensed version of the blurb – and the price of the book. The purpose of this catalogue is only to boost the sales of the book and so the negative aspects, if any, that are likely to adversely affect the sales of the book, are totally suppressed, highlighting only its positive side. These catalogues, which are now published mostly by the publishers themselves and are called publisher's catalogues or lists, were, in early years, published by booksellers.

The library catalogue, no doubt, has certain features similar to both, the list and the inventory, but it is basically different from both of them and the difference lies in the objectives and structures of these three tools. And while the library catalogue has a standardised structure, the structures of the other two varies according to the requirements of the individuals, organisations or institutions concerned. Although catalogues of both the library and the publisher target readers, the library catalogue differs fundamentally from a publisher's catalogue too, for the library catalogue looks at readers as readers and researchers while the publisher's catalogue treats readers merely as customers. To put it differently, the library catalogue views a book as encapsulated information while the publisher's catalogue deals with it as a commodity. And no library catalogue gives the biodata of the author. Hence, although it is more akin to a publisher's catalogue than to a simple list or inventory, it differs from that too as the purpose of these two types of catalogues are totally different.

Unlike a list or an inventory, and even a publisher's catalogue, the objectives of the library catalogue, as enunciated by Cutter (Cutter, 1904), are:

(i) to enable a reader to locate a particular book or, in the context of today, we must say any informational material, in the library, if the author, title or subject of the book is known;

(ii) to tell the reader what the library has by a given author, on a given subject in the case of informative literature and in a given genre of imaginative literature; and

(iii) to help the reader, particularly the researcher for whom it is very important, to know the edition and the distinctive features of the book

The International Conference on Cataloguing Principles held in 1961 at Paris has repeated practically the functions that Cutter had enumerated and those are, (i) to enable a user to find out whether the library has a given book by a given author or title and what all books by a particular author are in the library. If, however, the author's name is not given in the book, the user should be enabled to get at the book by its title alone and if author and title are inappropriate or insufficient for identification a substitute for the title should be given.

Strangely, both Cutter and the International Conference have overlooked the possibility of a user wanting to find out what all books on a particular subject are available in the library and this is very important for a researcher or a student who is interested in a particular discipline. This lacuna was noticed by S.R.Ranganathan who pointed it out, stating "if it is interest in a subject that takes him (the patron) to the library, his wants will be better served if the catalogue can spread before him a full, connected panorama of all the materials on his specified subject, all its sub-divisions and all broader subjects of which it is itself a sub-division."

(Ranganathan, 1964) And this lacuna can be filled only by a classified catalogue.

Cataloguing, in the library, is the process of recording the bibliographical details of the books in the collection, giving each of them its unique call number that will indicate to the user the location of the item in the library thereby enabling him to pick up the material that he wants without any difficulty or delay. The catalogue, in addition, helps the user to know what works by a particular author the library has, if the library has a certain book of a given author, if it has a book of a given title, what all books on a particular subject are available in the library and in which shelf each item is to be found. The catalogue should also tell the user if the library has on its shelf a book of a translator, editor or compiler. Now, thanks to the computerisation of the catalogue, the reader is able to get this information with just one click. It is, therefore, essential that every library should have a comprehensive catalogue that tells the user all this information. In addition to these, the catalogue necessarily gives the reader, complete bibliographical details like the number of volumes, the publisher's name, the year of publication, the number of pages in the case of univolume editions, if the book is illustrated or not, the series to which the book belongs and the size of the book. Hence no book added to the collection should find a place on the shelf of the library without being catalogued so that it could be traced by the user without wasting his time.

The cataloguing process is not confined to books alone, for, today, the library – be it big, medium-sized or small – stocks various other instructional materials. And even printed documents include materials other than books, like for example newspapers, journals, music scores, pamphlets, clippings, pictures and such other materials. Apart from these, the library is expected to stock photographs, prints and maps as well as machine-readable data files, motion pictures, microfilms, film strips, sound recordings, audio/ video tapes, CDs and DVDs. Besides all these, many libraries, particularly children's libraries, keep three dimensional materials like realia, globes, and various working models. Desirably, toys too! All these also have to be catalogued, in the interest of service to the clientele. Be it a book or non-book material, cataloguing is not just a mechanical work that any typist can do and which does not call for any thinking or technical knowledge as the layman is prone to think. On the other hand, it is a time-consuming intellectual and technical work that has to be done with utmost care, without committing any error in the entries and it involves the labour of not less than four to five hands, professional, clerical and unskilled. Besides, it has been estimated by the Library of Congress that to catalogue a typical book not less than three to five hours are required.

The process of cataloguing has two aspects. The first is that of descriptive cataloguing which fixes the identity of the book or the item concerned by describing it and determining its Main Entry that contains the fullest particulars of the item and giving Added Entries for editor, translator, title, subjects and any other relevant matter. The other is that of subject cataloguing that constitutes assigning Subject Heading, which is the term denoting the subject that the book deals with and giving a Call Number or the number that may consist of only digits or a combination of digits and letters that helps the user to locate the book or item on the shelf. The call number, of course, is the symbolic representation of the subject and the author (in the case of the Decimal Classification) or the year of publication (in the case of the Colon Classification) of the book.

There are different types of catalogues – Book Catalogue, Sheaf Catalogue, Card Catalogue, Computer Output Microform (COM) and Cathode Ray Tube (CRT) or Visual Display Terminal (VDT). In addition to these, there are two types of LAN catalogues, like peer-to-peer network catalogue and client-server network catalogue.

Of these, the book catalogue was the earliest form of catalogue that was designed by librarians and had been in use for a long time but is no more in vogue except, perhaps, in some village libraries in our country, which are starved of funds and lack professional hands to manage. In the book catalogues entries were made in page form and when leaves were bound, catalogues of libraries with large collections, became bulky tomes. Owing to the difficulty in handling this and the possibility of getting various subjects mixed up, the librarians conceived the divided catalogue and bound them into several volumes, each volume representing one subject. However, this did not solve the main problem. Whether a unified catalogue or a divided catalogue, when it was in book form, new entries could not be added as new items were added to the library collection, with the result the catalogue became out of print by the time it came out of the press. In other words, the drawback with this was the difficulty in updating it regularly. So after a year or so, a new edition of the catalogue was to be brought out with the entries of subsequent additions. In order to avoid frequent reprinting, the libraries tried bringing out printed catalogues interleaved with blank sheets so that later additions could be written on the blank interleaves. Even this was difficult for readers to consult because very soon the alphabetical order of the entries on the interleaves got jumbled and so the practice of issuing supplements of typed or printed sheets of new additions was tried out. It had many advantages but the frequent preparation of manuscript and proof reading involved considerable labour and with all that it would be out of print when it was ready for use. So that too failed to solve the problem.

Many libraries, therefore, preferred the sheaf catalogue to the book form of catalogue. This was similar to book form but the entries were typed on thin, loose sheets of paper of 7-1/2" by 4". These sheets were punched on one side and bound into handy volumes, each volume generally containing about 500 to 600 leaves. This was more flexible than the book catalogue, for new entries could be inserted periodically, though with difficulty as the binders had to be unlocked, many sheaves would have to be removed and after inserting the sheaf with the new entry, the removed sheaves had to be replaced without disturbing the order and the binder locked again.

This has, therefore, been given up in favour of the card catalogue, which is still in vogue in our country today, though being gradually pushed out by the computerised catalogue. The card catalogue is akin to the sheaf catalogue with the difference that instead of the loose sheets of paper, this has cards, which are much easier and more convenient to handle than sheets of paper. The size of the card has been standardised since 1901 – its length being 12.5 cm, width 7.5 cm and thickness 0.025 cm. These cards may be arranged in trays and held in position by rods that can be easily inserted through the holes at bottom centre in the cards and removed whenever required, the trays being placed in a cabinet. The rods preclude the possibility of any card getting lost or misplaced by users while looking through them. This cabinet of trays containing the cards is kept in an easily accessible place, usually at the entrance of the stack room, where the readers can consult the catalogue conveniently.

In a library catalogue, each item should have at least three entries with these three headings – author, title and subject – as access points. And in the case of books that have other possible access points, like translator, editor, and/or compiler besides series, there should be entries with those headings also. In the case of card catalogues, there had to be a card for each access point. On the other hand, in computerised catalogues, just one single file of catalogue data is enough as it contains all information needed in a catalogue and could be so programmed that the user would be able to retrieve the entries of items through all important file points or access points.

Strangely, after the advent of the computer and networking of libraries, it is often heard being said that cataloguers are an endangered species and cataloguing is on its deathbed. If the cataloguer had not vanished from the US, with the introduction of centralised cataloguing in that country in the early twentieth century, the cataloguers can rest assured that they are not an imperilled species. The Library of Congress had started to catalogue books that were being published and to distribute cards in 1901. Since 1956, with the enactment of Library Services Act, several centres for processing library materials were established and two years later, the idea of cataloguing-in-source was tried out, according to which, based on the proof of a book that were received from the publisher, the main entry was printed in the book. So each library that purchased a book would not have to spend time cataloguing it; hence there was no need for many cataloguers, however big the library was. This was, for some reason, found to be unsatisfactory and so the Library of Congress began to obtain galley proofs from publishers and printed the catalogue entry in full on the back of the title page. For example, the catalogue entry for *Jesus Lived in India* by Holger Kersten, given in the book, is as follows (See Fig.2).

As Barnett points out, "in the hand crafting of bibliographies involving a professional, a clerk-typist and a supervisor, careful attention to the placement and spelling of each word and actual handling of the item, seems almost quaint today" and he states, "over the last twenty years, we have witnessed the end of this system. Catalogue departments have transmuted into Processing or Technical Services units, with a much-diminished professional presence. Items are now rarely catalogued but much more often processed, with the bibliographic record selected with little or no reference to the physical item. It is, at its base, now a clerical rather than an intellectual process, a matter of properly shifting a digital record from one network to another." (Barnett, 2002). This is, no doubt, true in the

Fig. 2

Library of Congress Cataloguing

Kersten, Holger

Jesus lived in India: his unknown life before and after his crucifixion / Holger Kersten.

p. cm.

Translated from the German.

Includes bibliographical references and indexes.

ISBN 1-85230-550-9 9pbk.) $ 14.95 (U.S.)

1. Jesus Christ—biography. 2. Jesus Christ—Rationalistic interpretations. 3. India—History—Religious aspects—Christianity. I. Title

BT303.K47 1994

232.9'01—dc 20

[B] 94—33959 CIP

---

case of developed countries, which have automated and networked libraries and sooner rather than later it will be true of developing countries too. Nevertheless, neither the cataloguer nor cataloguing would get extinct as long as libraries exist because catalogue is an inevitable tool of the library, without which it is not possible for the library to function. Even if all the books are microfilmed or even if all printed books are replaced by e-books, a catalogue is essential and there cannot be a catalogue without a cataloguer. The computer cannot replace the cataloguer, for no computer but a cataloguer, rather a trained cataloguer, alone can assign subject headings.

No doubt, cataloguers may vansih from many libraries and get concentrated in the central library and cataloguing technique, as we have known it hitherto is bound to change, maybe beyond recognition, just as the library of today is not the library of yesteryears and the library of tomorrow will not be the library of today. It will only be a wonder if such changes do not take place, for everything changes and nothing remains static. As Heraclitus, the Greek philosopher, had said, "one cannot step twice into the same river;" hence it is but natural that the library and library techniques change as much as the cataloguer and cataloguing technique. And a progressive librarian ought to be happy that it changes, for it shows that the institution of library is keeping in step with the developments taking place in the world around and has not become deadwood. In fact, if it does not change, it will affect the efficacy of library services and the *raison d'être* for such an institution may be called into question.

Interestingly, with the computer entering the library, it is not the cataloguer that has become redundant but all other types of catalogue including the card catalogue as well as the method of preparing catalogue. This work, which had all these years been done manually, either with a pen or with a typewriter, began to be done with a computer. This helps save considerable time and labour, with the result the services of the cataloguer can be utilised for readers' guidance or 'floor work', to use an American term. The computer can be used for preparing both the book catalogue as well as the card catalogue (Swihart, 1973). The former, either unified or divided, can be brought out in any desired format, like for example straight columnar format or indented columnar format and a simple author or title catalogue with the names of authors or titles of books in alphabetical order with the call number against each, in key-only format, provided there is another catalogue giving all the data about the book concerned. Similarly, the computer can be used to prepare the card catalogue. Swihart points out the various kinds of clerical work that can be done with the computer. Those are, (a) assembling and arranging the data on the card, (b) generating automatically the access point or file point based upon the data on the card, (c) positioning the access point at the top of the card, (d) printing of as many copies as are required of the card and (e) arranging the cards in alphabetical order making it easy for the librarian to interfile into the card catalogue, in their proper places.

The computer, thus, enables the librarian to have the catalogue card printed in any format that he wants. The format of a catalogue card of a school library or a children's public library has to be very different from that of the library of a research institute, which again may not be the same as that of an adult public library. The content and the layout of the card can be programmed to meet the specific demands of the library concerned. There is another advantage in the library having such machine-readable master files. If the Library Committee takes a policy decision to change the system of classification hitherto being followed to another that the Committee feels would be better in the interest of the patrons, the process of conversion – be it for example from Colon to Dewey or *vice versa* – can be carried out in a matter of a few days, once the necessary programming is done, which may, of course, take a few weeks.

When the catalogue is computerised, the entire file is stored in the computer and so, actually, there is no need to take hard copies of the catalogue either in book format or in card format, if the catalogue is meant for that library alone, i.e. if it is not a part of any co-operative cataloguing project, like for example, the Online Computer Library Centre (OCLC) in the US or the University of Toronto Library Automation System (UTLAS) in Canada, about which we shall be discussing a little later. The readers can consult the catalogue directly from the computer itself, in which the data is stored;

hence a book form catalogue or a card catalogue is redundant. But the problem is that the entire catalogue is in one computer, which can be consulted by one person only at a time and the others who want to consult the catalogue will have to wait in queue, for it is not possible to have split catalogue – separate subject, author and title catalogues – as can be done in the case of book form catalogue or card catalogue. This difficulty can be obviated by installing the local area network (LAN), either peer-to-peer network or client-server network catalogue, in the library, provided the library has sufficient funds to meet the cost of the computers and installation charges. However, once it is installed there will be no problem. The catalogue may also be linked to the circulation system and can be programmed to display, apart from the bibliographic details of the item, location (if the library has more than one unit), the media, the date of issue and the due date if the book is on loan, the identity of the borrower and the reservation status.

Of the two, the former is better, particularly for small libraries in which less than twelve computers only are required. There seems to be very high level of user satisfaction with peer-to-peer network catalogues than with card catalogues. In this system, all computers are, so to speak, 'peers' or of equal status, functioning both as servers and clients or workstations, as the clients are called; there is no dedicated file server. Nevertheless, it can be so configured that the one in which all the data that are required for the accession register are fed can be the server which may share the data needed for the catalogue alone or whatever the Chief Librarian wants to share with the 'peers' that act as clients. In such an arrangement too, the network is peer-to-peer because every computer on the network may be administered individually. The advantages of this system over the client-server network are many. This operates on single operating system and does not need a network operating system (NOS); nor is any special and elaborate training required for the user to administer this. The computers' resources are controlled by the users concerned and the resources are administered by the owner of each client computer or workstation.

The client-server network, on the other hand, has a dedicated file server computer, which provides resources and is not used as a client or workstation and the other computers, which are all clients, only use the resources. Besides, this system, being more advanced and complex with more security options, is more expensive and difficult to install and administer. Nevertheless, this is more advantageous than peer-to-peer network as under this system more workstations can be handled simultaneously. For example, if there is more than one circulation area, under the client-server network books can be issued from all those counters simultaneously, which is not possible with peer-to-peer network.

It was in 1966 that the idea of co-operative cataloguing arose. Automation of libraries started in the 1960s and six years later, sixteen libraries in the US joined and launched the machine-readable catalogue (MARC) project. They designed a standard format for electronic version of the card catalogue, and the work involved in creating records for the electronic catalogue was shared by all the participants of the project. By 1972, many libraries around the world contributed to this project resulting in the development of MARC II. This made it possible to enter at any point the details of a document, which could then be transmitted to a central data file. The other libraries can obtain from this, the details by means of telecommunication links. This idea of co-operative cataloguing soon caught on and organisations like the Ohio College Library Centre, later came to be known as the OCLC, which was a computer network of catalogues of the University and colleges of Ohio, came into being, followed by some others like the Research Library and Information Network (RLIN) in the US and the UTLAS in Canada. As a consequence of the organisation of these centres, all items procured by them are catalogued only once and no other library that is a part of any of these organisations needs to repeat the task of cataloguing them, thus saving the time and labour of all those libraries. The OCLC eventually grew into a 'Bibliographic Utility,' which is what a large organisation that shares catalogues with one another, is called. This has extended its services beyond the borders of the US.

In spite of all the advantages that a computer-generated card catalogue may have over a book form catalogue or even a manually prepared card catalogue, it is certainly inferior to a computer output microform (COM) catalogue. This format is new but not the process. This is the process by which the data created by a computer in digital form is converted to an analog signal that modifies an energy source exposing a microimage on 16mm/35mm film or 105x148mm microfiche; it can be 35mm chips also. Its advantages are: (a) it can be placed even outside of the library; (b) author, title and subject entries can be on separate films; (c) it is possible to view several records at one time. Above all, the equipment is not very expensive. Nonetheless, this has quite a few defects: (i) it cannot be updated easily; hence peridocial supplements have to be brought out and the user may have to look into several files; (ii) deleted entries remain in the file till the next upadte, confusing the user (iii) a microfilm reader/printer is necessary to copy entries; (iv) microfilm may not often be as clear as print;

The computerised catalogue of which the entire data on the master file can be displayed on the television screen, known as the on-line public access computer (OPAC) is the latest innovation in cataloguing. In this technique, the information is stored in a computer memory and displayed on a television screen called CRT terminal or visual display terminal (VDT). As nowadays, VDT may also indicate, a plasma display or liquid crystal display, we shall stick to the term CRT terminal display. This basically comprises a display monitor, a keyboard, a control unit and a controller, to which may be added a printer, a communications interface and such other peripherals. (See Fig. 3)

Fig. 3
CRT Terminal

```
                              {Key Board}
                                   ^            → {Printer}
                                   |            |
{CRT     }  {CRT     }             v            v
{Display }← {Control} ←→ {Micro Processor} ←→ {Communications Interface}
{Monitor }  {Unit    }                          ^
                                                |
                                                → {Other Peripherals}
```

This, of course, is too expensive for libraries, which run on modest budgets. However, public libraries managed by State Governments, the National Library, Kolkata, Connemara Library, Chennai, Asiatic Library, Mumbai, University Libraries, libraries of research institutes, special libraries, Raja Rammohun Roy Library, many college libraries, libraries of Public, International, Central and Sainik Schools, Navodaya Vidyalayas and quite a few affluent private schools should be able to afford OPAC. And it will be advantageous if they have inter-library loan system too.

This system is now quite developed, making it possible to integrate other library functions and records with OPAC. The users can reserve a book that is on order and also know if a book is on loan. The OPAC can also include information about articles in journals and even about the community that the library serves. In short, the work of the cataloguer today is not confined to describing the materials in the library; he is an information disseminator producing an information retrieval tool that will provide the patrons all sorts of information.

Although catalogues of collections were made even in the libraries of the ancient world, the rules regarding its format and the information that it is expected to provide had not been codified then. This may be because in those days, the librarians were concerned solely with the security and maintenance of the collection, as the library, then, was more a depository than a service organisation, unlike it is in modern times. The revival of literature during the Ranaissance resulted in the establishment of many libraries and brought about decisive changes in the philosophy of library service, reflecting the ethos of the times, which necessitated standardisation of the catalogue format. Besides, after the invention of printing, books began to be produced in larger numbers than ever before. The construction of all-metal press in England at the fag end of the 18th century increased the printing capacity of the press. But the advent of Industrial Revolution (roughly 1750 to 1850) and the expansion of education resulting from the needs of the newly established colonies for skilled and educated workers gave an impetus to the printing industry. Thanks to Friedrich Koenig of Germany, the early 19th century witnessed improved technique "in which the raising and lowering of the platen, the to-and-fro movement of the bed and the inking of the form by a series of rollers were controlled by a system of gear wheels." Consequent upon this, there was an unprecedented proliferation of books and the collections in libraries grew immensely. Coupled with this, and with the growing demand for reading materials, the need for devising a standard form of the catalogue became an urgent necessity.

The first serious attempt at standardisation of the catalogue was made by Anthony Panizzi, who was appointed Assistant librarian in 1831 and on promotion worked, as Principal Librarian from 1856 to 1866 at the British Museum. This catalogue code consisting of ninety-one rules, called the British Museum Code, which had appeared in 1841, was revised several times, the last revision being in 1936. Being the first catalogue code, it had its influence on all codes[2] that were produced subsequently although almost all of them had deviated considerably from it. However, let us take a peep into it. Panizzi had framed these rules keeping in mind only the British Museum and as a result, he prefers the English form of names in all cases, including those of ancient Greek writers, kings, popes and saints. In the case of books having two authors, he recommends that the heading should contain the names of both and if there are more than two, the first name alone should form the heading. When cataloguing translations, the main entry must be under the name of the original writer with an added entry for the translator. And for compound names, Panizzi prefers entry generally to be under the first part of the name but under the second part in the case of English and Dutch names. Pseudonyms are to be entered under that followed by real names in square brackets and the names of married women are to be entered under the maiden name with a reference to the one adopted after marriage. Anonymous ones are entered under the first word of the title, disregarding the article. For example, if the title of the book is "The Organisation of Libraries", the access point should be "Organisation" and not "The". Encyclopaedias, Directories and Almanacs are to be entered under the form headings. While 'series' are recommended to be entered under the name of the editor, if it is given, all annual publications are to be under the heading, "Periodical Publications". As far as government publications are concerned, he suggests to use the name of the country, state or city as the case may be as access point and similarly, institutions, including national and those named after celebrities, will have the names of the places where they are situated, as access points. International societies are to be entered under the names of the parent countries and other societies under the names of the places where the headquarters are located.

The next catalogue code that made its appearance was the A. A. Code or the American Library Association Code, which was brought out in 1883. The understanding arrived at between the Library Association of London and the American Library Association fifteen years later was, perhaps, the first international attempt at bringing about uniformity of cataloguing practice. This dealt with the author and title entries only and was the widely acclaimed Anglo-American *Catalogue Rules; Author and Title Entries.* First published in 1908, it was revised twice, first in 1967 and again in 1978 and was known as *Anglo-American Cataloguing Rules*, the second edition being referred to as *AACR2.* Apart from these, there are other codes like Cutter's Rules for a Dictionary Catalogue, the Vatican Code prescribing rules for the cataloguing of printed books, the Prussian Instructions codifying rules for the alphabetical catalogues of Prussian libraries and the Classified Catalogue Code of Ranganathan. Among all these, the most extensively used code is the AACR2.

A card-catalogue record in a research library, according to AACR2 will be almost as given in Fig. 4. But all these details are not necessary in all other types of libraries. Perhaps, in a university library, this may be useful but not in a public library or even in the library of a college that does not have students working for doctorate degrees. And no librarian who is sane would incorporate all these details in the catalogue of a children's library.

Fig. 4.

Main Entry as per AACR2

Blackburn, Robin. <u>Ed</u>

Ideology in social science: readings in critical social theory / ed. by Robin Blackburn – 3rd ed. – Glasgow: Collins (c) 1975.

XV, 382 p. ; 18cm

Essays first published in New Left Review, Towards Socialism, Canadian Journal of Economcs, The Antioch Review, Diogenes and Socialist Register.

Includes Index.

ISBN 0-00-632891-1.

1. Politics. 2. Sociology. 3. Anthropology. 4. Economics. 5. History.

We have seen that library catalogue has been evolving both in form and content, the former in step with the developing library technology and the latter depending upon the clientele expected to use the library. And all these changes are for the benefit of the readers. So whatever is the physical form, the function of the catalogue is to inform the reader,

* what books the library has by a particular author;
* if the library has a certain book of a given author/ translator/editor/compiler;
* if the library has a book of a given title;
* what books the library has on a particular discipline;

and

* which all books contain information on a particular subject.

It follows from this that the catalogue should give detailed information like the author, title, edition and the year of publication. Besides, it should also give bibliographical information such as the number of volumes, if it is a multi-volume publication, the number of pages in the case of a single-volume publication, illustrations, size of the book and the name of the series to which the book belongs. Above all, it must show the location of the book on the shelf and this, of course, is indicated by the Call Number, which presupposes that all books have to be classified prior to being catalogued. The catalogues of all types of libraries, except children's, have to have profuse analytical entries. There may be some among the clientele of other types of libraries, who are engaged in research. And it is possible to direct them to all the books that have information on the subjects that they are interested in, only with the help of such analytical entries, for the librarian cannot depend on his memory for it. In fact, even in children's libraries a few analytical entries are imperative, for these days, many children come to the library with doubts, which neither the teacher nor the librarian would be able to clear. So they may have to be directed to the books, which give the information that they are looking for. A children's librarian, of schools and juvenile public libraries, from her experience would know the kind of queries that children usually come up with and analytical entries can be made in the catalogue accordingly. In the school library catalogue, many more analytical entries than in that of the juvenile public library, may be required depending upon the curriculum.

Nevertheless, catalogues in all types of libraries need not give such detailed information. It is, indubitably, necessary in a research library or even in a university library. But such details are certainly not required in the catalogues of school libraries or children's public libraries – why, even in adult public libraries. So the Chief Librarian has to formulate the cataloguing policy depending on the clientele of the library and adopt selective and simplified catalogues in libraries excluding such details that are not necessary.

Footnotes

1 A brief history of the catalogue (Beckmann, 1846) is given in Appendix 2.

2 As such, Panizzi's code is comparable to the Napoleanic Code of Civil Laws enacted in 1804, which had been the main influence for the civil codes of all European and Latin American countries.

9
Managerial Duties

The American Library Association defines management as "the process of co-ordinating the total resources of an organisation toward the accomplishment of the desired goals of that organisation through the execution of a group of inter-related functions such as planning, organising, staffing, directing and controlling. So defined, management is usually used synonymously with administration in current literature. Administration may be considered to be a broader term, emphasising the planning function, involving goal setting and major policy formulations, with management variously limited to the process of co-ordinating certain functions and activities of an organisation toward the accomplishment of its goals." (Young, H., 1983.)

The managerial control of a company vests in the Board of Directors, that of a University in the Academic Council, of a Public Library in the Local Government or the Ministry of Education, of an academic or a special library in the institution or organisation of which it is an appendage. The controlling authority formulates a body of rules, regulations, policies, procedures, guidelines and objectives for the whole organisation and the library, which is a part of it operates within those specified parameters and limits. As Evans puts it, the "administrators establish fundamental patterns of operations and goals for an organisation, while managers primarily carry out the directions of the administrators." (Evans, 1983.). Any establishment, therefore, is run by a manager or a team of managers within the framework of the policy and strategy set by the Board, which also appoints the manager or the team of managers with one designated as general manager to head the team.

The general manager is expected to carry out the policies and programmes of the Board and achieve the target that has been set for him. He cannot, obviously, do it by himself but has to get it done with the help of the team of managers and supported by many technical and clerical staff that the Board of Directors has provided him with. Management, therefore, is the art of achieving a target set by the Board, with the help of the group of skilled and unskilled hands that work under the guidance and supervision of a team of managers, the general manager acting as the co-ordinator. The main function of the management, as Sharma puts it pithily is "not 'to do' but how to get work done". (Sharma, 1995). As such, the manager has to see that work is done, which presupposes that the manager necessarily has to be good at man-management, which calls for sagacity, perspicacity, resourcefulness and above all, tact.

Understandably, any group-work needs someone to co-ordinate and to supervise the work to ensure that it goes on smoothly in the desired direction and achieves the target as planned, within the specified time limit. The manager of course, is not a modern phenomenon. Even in olden days, the need for a person to manage group work had been realised but the managers of those days were basically different from what they are today. In ancient India, when the Aryan tribes came into this sub-continent as immigrants, they lived in communes, which were non-hierarchical and egalitarian socio-economic organisations. When there was any work in a commune that had to be carried out by a group of persons or the entire commune, all the members of the commune were – as could be deduced from myths and mythical rites – 'elected to temporary functional roles' (Dange, 1951).

During this time, there would naturally be one person elected to supervise and co-ordinate the work, very much like what the general manager of a company – in the context of a library, the chief librarian – does today. Obviously, therefore, this person corresponds to the manager or the general manager of today. But he was not paid for the work he does as the manager. And, no sooner the work in the commune was completed, than the functionaries reverted to their original roles as ordinary members of equal status in the commune. So in those days, unlike as it is today, there were none acting as managers on a permanent basis, appointed and paid by a superior authority and whoever acted as a manager was elected by the group the work of which he supervised and co-ordinated. In other words, the managers of yesteryears were one of those belonging to the group and the person acting as manager at one time may or may not be the manager the next time. The manager of modern times, on the contrary, is a permanent appointee imposed on the group from above and the group he would be supervising has no voice in his selection. More than anything else the acceptance of the person acting as the manager by the group was the primary factor, then. Today, on the other hand, the acceptance of the person acting as the manager by the group that he supervised is not considered necessary at all; what is imperative is the acceptance of the manager by the Board. The manager today is not a representative of the group but a representative of the Board, which appoints him and to which alone he is responsible.

As, today, the society itself is split into hierarchical strata, it is but natural that the structure of a company or any corporate organisation would inevitably be a reflection of that. So understandably every organisation, big or small, is run by an hierarchy, at the apex of which, depending upon the size and nature of the organisation, there is the general manager, under whom, there may be one or more deputy managers. Each of these deputy managers may have, under him, one or more assistant managers and all these assistant managers may have supervisors below them. And it goes on until it reaches the base, which would be a large team of supporting staff comprising the clerks as well as the skilled and unskilled labourers. Each level may have its own supporting staff also. The general manager of a gigantic company like the Tata's or the Reliance, normally, may not have much direct contact with the levels below that of the deputy managers of the organisation although there is a remote possibility of a few making it a point to know those at lower levels. It is a sort of an iron-clad pyramidal structure, as it were. The general manager directs and unifies the group and his directives, passed from tier to tier down to the bottom, are carried out, each tier being monitored by the managerial team of that tier. Over and above the general manager who is only a paid employee, in large organisations, there could be a Managing Director or President, elected by the owners or directors from among themselves, who has financial stakes in the company and the general manager is the interface between him and the executive staff.

The managerial team, each member of which would be a specialist in a particular field of management – like for example, personnel, finance, marketing and so on – is controlled and led by the general manager. So is the case with the library. In the context of a library, the chief librarian (or the librarian in the case of a library being managed by only one professionally qualified person) corresponds to the general manager and the managerial team comprises other professional librarians each of whom would be managing a particular technical section. Howsoever big a library is, there would be no immediate boss corresponding to the managing director of a company. In any matter connected exclusively with the library, the administration is expected to consult the chief librarian and act on his advice. As far as public libraries are concerned, the Ministry of Education acts in consultation with the Director (or *ex officio* Director) of Libraries who is the overall manager of all public libraries in the State.

There are, however, two fundamental differences between the general manager of a company and the chief librarian. The general manager of a company, like for example a pharmaceutical company, may be a graduate or a post-graduate in economics, management or in any discipline but not necessarily that which has a bearing on the commodities that the company manufactures. As such he need not have basic theoretical knowledge of pharmacology or even chemistry; nor should he have any idea of the process of manufacturing the various drugs that the company produces. There are technically qualified production manager and his team of technical assistants who have the knowledge and necessary expertise to take care of those aspects. No doubt, as general manager he would be able to contribute substantially to the company's advancement if he had at least a minimum theoretical knowledge of the compositions and the production processes of the commodities that the company brings out.

Such a situation is unthinkable in a library. The chief librarian, who occupies a position corresponding to the general manager of a company, has to be an accredited librarian – a person who has qualified himself in the profession of librarianship. In fact, appointing a non-professional as chief librarian of a library is like putting a person who has not undergone a course in civil engineering, in charge of constructing a bridge. The results in both these cases could be predicted – the bridge will not stay to serve its purpose and the library will not achieve its objectives! Besides, unlike the general manager of a big company, he is, at the same time, the personnel manager, financial manager, technical manager-in-chief, marketing manager ('marketing' in reference to the library is 'selling', in the figurative sense, books to the readers) as well as the pubic relations officer. Of course, it is incumbent on the assistant librarians also to share the burden of 'marketing' and public relations while the other areas of management are entirely the concern of the chief librarian. In fact, the chief librarian or any librarian for that matter should pay more attention to 'marketing' than to anything else.

If a bureaucrat from the Indian Administrative Service, for example, is put in charge of a library, he will be an utter failure because he is an out-and-out administrator and in his perception efficient administration is the be-all and end-all of an organisation. Hence he will be concentrating on administration to the detriment of service to the clientele in particular and the community in general, thus defeating the very purpose of the library. On the other hand, a professional librarian as chief librarian would consider administration as just a means to effective service to the community. This does not imply he will be neglecting administration; he will streamline the administration towards the main objective of the library: *service*. That is, *service to the clientele* and *service to the community*. To him, administration is just a means to that end. The library being basically, as repeatedly stated in earlier chapters, a service institution, the chief librarian ensures that the entire team of professional librarians and the non-professional personnel is geared to this end. And like any committed librarian, he is aware that his primary duty is service to the clientele and the community and his managerial duties are only subordinate to that.

At the same time, he knows, efficient and systematic management is the desideratum for effective service. No doubt, as pointed out in Chapter 1, 'Librarianship in India', it would be desirable if he had an idea of the fundamentals of management, for in a way, all librarians are managers. In a small library, there would be only one professional librarian and he is the manager like that of a small-scale business organisation. No library, howsoever small it may be, can be managed by one professional librarian alone. There has to be at least a clerical assistant and needless to say an attendant cum sweeper. This is the minimum strength of the staff required even in a library serving a very small community in a remote rural area where the need to carry out the extension service aimed at spreading literacy and education is all the greater than in a town or outskirts of a town. Although the library in such a locality is small in terms of resources and membership, the librarian of that library also, like the chief librarian of a big library, is constrained to act as the general manager, the financial, personnel, technical, and 'marketing' manager besides public relations officer as well. And in addition to all that if he has to function effectively as an engineer of educational development and social change, which is absolutely necessary in a community like that, a helper is imperative.

The chief librarian, using his and his assistants' technical know-how, gets the documents and other stock-in-trade like, for example pamphlets, periodicals, clippings, graphic and electronic materials in the library arranged in such a way that the reader will be able to access whatever material he needs or retrieve any information that he seeks with the least difficulty. He would also ensure that all electronic and other audio-visual materials are properly maintained and are in working condition. If anything is found in disrepair, he will get it set right expeditiously. Metaphorically speaking, as Dr. Ralph puts it, he 'keeps the wheels of the apparatus oiled and turning'. And if the reader faces any problem with the machinery, the librarian with his technical knowledge is always at hand to help fix up and make it possible for him to find what he is looking for. The means by which the chief librarian as the technical manager has to keep the library in such good working condition as well as what he does as the 'marketing' manager, has been dealt with in detail in the relevant chapters.

In his capacity as the financial manager, his duty is the presentation of the budget to the controlling authority and to ensure that the expenditure is kept within the budgetary allotment. The library, whether public, academic or special, may be compared to any of the government departments as far as its finances are concerned. The public library of course, being an institution run directly by the government gets its annual budgetary allotment from the government. The funds for a library attached to a government school or college are drawn out of the total annual budget of the parent institution. In the case of a government school the headmaster, usually, discusses the budgetary proposals put up by the librarian at the school library committee[1] meeting specially convened for the purpose, when the allocation for the library is decided and this amount is included in the school budget. In many colleges, the principal in consultation with the librarian decides upon the annual allotment required for the library and for university libraries, the authorities of the university concerned with the finance allots the amount on the basis of the budgetary proposals put up by the university librarian. But every quasi-government or non-government library depends on funds appropriated by the administrative authority under which it operates. In most cases, the library budget includes the outlay for binding and maintenance. In the case of some special libraries, like for example the libraries of Research and Development sections of certain industrial firms, the allotment for libraries is earmarked exclusively for the purchase of books and periodicals as well as other resources like the cassettes or CDs/DVDs, the expenditure on binding and maintenance being debited to some other head of account. Usually, if the library needs to purchase a computer or any such expensive equipment, the librarian makes a separate demand for an *ad hoc* grant to the administrative authority concerned.

The chief librarian has also the responsibility to allot duties to professional assistants, clerks and other members of the staff as well as to supervise their work. The library is, in a way, comparable to a corporate establishment and in any such corporate body, human resources constitute an important factor. The success or failure of the establishment depends on its personnel. The chief librarian should realise that if he succeeds in building up a good collection, in providing facilities for the readers to read and research and in automating all sections of the library, it is in no small measure – why, in full measure – due to his co-workers.[2] Proper personnel management is very important if the chief librarian wants his colleagues, professional and non-professional, to give of their best, which alone would ensure success in achieving the objectives of the library. In short, this, the success or failure in achieving the objectives of course, depends on the entire staff. The objectives, needless to say, vary from one type of library to another – for example, the objectives of the public library is totally different from those of the special library or those of the school library from those of the college library although both are academic libraries. The bottom line is, the chief librarian has to have a good rapport with the library personnel, for that would help him get the unstinted co-operation of the staff and make it easy for him to extract optimum work from the staff. The one and the only factor, that would enable him to secure such support and motivate his colleagues, is the human element.

And the crux of the human element is camaraderie. The chief librarian must regard the entire personnel not as men and women working *under* him but *with* him and his attitude should be such that they also feel they are working *with*, not *under*, him. This is imperative in order to make them consider themselves comrades and not underlings of the chief librarian. In other words, the chief librarian must view the rest of the staff as his team-mates and himself as the skipper of the team and deal with them in that spirit. And in fact, to a great extent his position is very much analogous to the captain of a football team. He has the responsibility to carry the members of the team with him while ensuring control over them. The captain as well as the chief librarian has to manage the players and allot each one his position on the field. No doubt, the captain has the coach to support and guide him but the chief librarian has to depend on himself alone. There is none to guide him.

In this connection, it must be pointed out that there is a pitfall, which the chief librarian has to be careful to avoid: the temptation to centralise control. This temptation is always great but that is exactly what the chief librarian should resist. A discussion of the merits and demerits of centralisation as against decentralisation is redundant here but suffice it to say that the advantages of decentralisation far outweigh those of centralisation. An intelligent chief librarian knows the advantages of decentralisation. He knows that it helps reduce considerably his burden of work with the result he has less tension and at the same time gives his colleagues a sense of belonging that would prove an incentive for them to work hard. He will also share responsibility and before taking any decision, including on the selection of resources, which is a very important work in any type of library, he takes into confidence and consults every member of the staff, even the junior most, irrespective of his age or lack of experience.

A good chief librarian holds staff meetings at regular intervals at which he discusses all matters connected with the work of the library with special reference to service, particularly extension service. At every meeting one of the items on the agenda should be problems faced by the members of the staff and if there are any, he should try to sort them out. All the items on the agenda must be discussed threadbare but he must be careful not to reveal what he has in his mind. Any difference of opinion or any dissenting voice should be listened to carefully and with due respect in true democratic spirit. In fact, he should encourage them to speak out without any hesitation, for possibly some of them may come out with some novel ideas that could be implemented in the library with advantage. He should take a final decision only after hearing and weighing the pros and cons of the various points of view. The ethos of democracy must be fully reflected in the working of the library and the chief librarian should refrain from taking any decision unilaterally. The decision that he takes may be what he had already decided upon but his colleagues get the feeling that he has been democratic in taking the decision. It helps make them feel they are wanted and are a part of the organisation. That will go a long way in enthusing the staff with the result they will work without any reservation.

At the same time he must remember that the five fingers of his hand are not alike; each is different from every other finger. And in the same way, each individual is different and *ipso facto* the abilities of each are also different. So he must treat each member of the staff *as what he is* and *not as what he should be* and the chief librarian can be sure that each of his colleagues, as he gains experience, will grow from what he is to what he should be. One of the colleagues who is zealous and hard working, for example, may not measure up to the expectation in work. He should not be condemned, for he deserves sympathetic guidance, given which he will, in course of time, show improvement. There are people who are good at their work but diffident and they need nothing but a few words of encouragement to overcome their nervousness. Even one who is competent but indifferent should not be reprimanded or talked down to, for that will help only in building a psychological barrier between him and the chief librarian. Instead, if handled with tact and understanding, it is possible to extract work from him commensurate with his competence. This does not mean that there is no one who has initiative and is efficient with necessary confidence to carry out independently the work given to him. Such a person may possibly be a little overbearing. Ignoring that, if he is handled patiently and tactfully his competence can be tapped to the fullest extent. As any personnel manager would testify, man management is the most difficult task and it is all the more so because there are no hard and fast rules that can be applied in the management of the personnel, which has to be according to a rule o' thumb only.

The next problem, that is allotting the right work to the right person, arises from this and is no less difficult than man-management; in fact, it is one of the aspects of man-management. This, in the case of the chief librarian of a public library, is all the more difficult because recruitment of the personnel is not usually made by him; nor is it done in consultation with him but by the controlling authority. He has to accept the material as it is and make the best of it. He can, however, take a cue from what the captain of the football team does in allotting positions. In a football team, the captain places the players in positions in which, he thinks, they will be able to play better than in any other position. A player who is good at the centre forward position is not asked to play as the 'left out' or to put it differently, one who plays well as full back may be a misfit as centre half. The captain watches the players during practice time and only then decides in what position each player has to be placed. So the chief librarian being the captain of the team should watch the members of his team at work and allot or re-allot work to each of them according to his competence and attitude to work. No one on the staff would be totally incompetent and inefficient; neither would they all be equally competent and efficient in all aspects of librarianship. One could be very good at cataloguing but poor at classifying, in which case he must be put in the cataloguing section. Unlike in the case of the captain of the football team, the chief librarian has to take into cognisance, a person's disposition also. A short-tempered person or a nervous person should never be put in a section, like for example the circulation or reference, where he has to deal with the clientele. So both ability and temperament of each of the members of the staff are to be taken into consideration when allotting duties to the staff. The chief librarian, therefore, has to be a good judge of men and he should be keenly and continually watching each member of the staff.

But it must be borne in mind that seldom does anyone remain at the same level of competence throughout his or her career, for as one gains experience one invariably progresses from the lower to the higher level of competence. At the same time, there could be one or two who do not show any improvement and some whose rate of improvement is rather slow; hence arises the necessity for periodical re-allotment of work. Those who have progressed must be made use of accordingly; those who are stagnant or slow must be given necessary support and guidance but never treated with disdain. Given time, they too are bound to show improvement.

As 'marketing' manager, the chief librarian has to organise publicity besides monitoring and guiding the work of the reference librarian and those in charge of extension services, both of which have been dealt with in separate chapters in detail. So here we shall discuss briefly what he has to do to give publicity to the resources available in the library and the services being rendered to the clientele. Many people would have known the extension service that the library has been undertaking and the benefits of it. The work he has to do in connection with publicity overlaps a great deal with what he would do as the Public Relations Officer. In organising and carrying out the extension services, as stated in chapter 5 'Extension Service' he would have already come in contact with the office bearers of the various organisations like the political parties, social service organisations, Rotary Club and such others that are operating in the town or village that forms the jurisdiction of the services of the library. And representatives of all such organisations would be coming to the library to attend the Library Extension Service Committee meetings. This opportunity may be made use of to acquaint them with the resources, both printed and electronic, of the library and the services being rendered to the clientele. Besides, copies of lists of latest additions to the library may be given to them to be displayed on the notice boards in their respective offices. The list to be given to each of these organisations should include only the titles of books that the members of the organisation concerned would be interested in. For example, titles of books on cookery, needle work and such other topics need not be included in the list intended for the Rotary Club but these must be included in the list being given to social service organisations. The librarian will use his sense of discrimination in preparing the lists. In addition to these, copies of the annual report of the library may be given to all those organisations for display on their office notice boards. Similarly, if he is a good 'marketing' manager, he will prepare posters about the library and put up in front of the library as well as distribute them to those organisations for display. He may also, occasionally visit the offices of organisations and give short talks about the library – the books that they would be interested in, the services that the library renders, the facilities to learn on their own and prepare for some examination that would help them get promotions or better jobs – and thus entice them to visit the library. A resourceful 'marketing' manager would be able to think of many other divers methods of publicity.

There are two basic registers that the chief librarian of every library has to maintain: (a) the accession register and. (b) the shelf-list. The former is the register of all the books that the library has procured and taken on stock. It must have columns for (i) date of accession, (ii) accession number, (iii) author, (iv) title, (v) publisher, (vi) year of publication and edition, (vii) vendor or donor (viii) invoice number and date, (ix) price, (x) call number and (xi) remarks. The last column is to note down when the book is withdrawn or lost. If it is paid for by the member who has lost it, the receipt number and date are to be noted. Accessioning may be done by the clerical assistant under the guidance of an assistant librarian (or the librarian, if there is only one professional librarian). The process of accessioning involves, collation (i.e., checking the book to see if there is any physical defect), putting the rubber stamp on the book, entering the particulars of the book in the accession register and the accession number in the book, pasting book-pocket, due date slip and book label. After the book is classified and catalogued, the book goes back to the accessioning clerk for entering the call number of the book in the relevant column and to prepare the shelf-list card.

The shelf-list is a (12.5x7.5 cm) card file of all the books in the library with the cards arranged in the same order in which the volumes are kept on the shelves. The flexibility of a card file weighs in its favour as against a loose-leaf form that some librarians suggest, in which several entries are made on the same page necessitating rewriting the whole page when it gets crowded by additions. So, indubitably, most librarians would opt for a card file only. The shelf-list card has columns for the call number, accession number, author and short title of the book. This is followed by a number of columns bearing the year to provide space for recording the status of the particular volume, when taking stock.

This raises the question of the need for stocktaking in a library. It may interest the librarians in our country to listen to what one distinguished librarian has to say about stock verification in a library: "Is stocktaking in fact ever to be undertaken? Is it necessary? At first sight these questions may seem foolish, but it is a fact that an increasing number of public librarians no longer undertake the task. It is laborious, occupying a large amount of time, even in a small library; borrowers are either completely excluded during the process or a vast amount of extra work is placed on the shoulders of the librarian and his staff. In the event, what purpose is served? It is discovered that certain volumes are totally missing. Yet surely in the case of any title of value to the collection this fact becomes evident during the course of the working year, merely by the process of a demand being made for it. From personal experience in control of a library issuing more than a million volumes a year, I would say categorically that stocktaking is a waste of valuable time and energy." (Leyland, 1961.) In short, stock verification in a library is nothing but an exercise in futility.

The success of the chief librarian, it must be understood, is not judged by the fact that no books are lost without trace; nor is it judged by the number of volumes in the shelves or by the appearance of the books therein. The facilities provided for the readers to make use of the books and the extent to which the books are used by the readers as well as the number of members and the extension services rendered are the touchstone of a library. In other words, the librarian knows or should know that the library is not merely a storehouse or museum of books but a centre for reading, self-education and research. So what is more important than managing the staff and keeping the library in trim, is the ability of the librarian to attract readers as well as facilitate recreational, informational and investigative reading, apart from carrying out the extension services that it is expected to render to the community. As Rabindranath Tagore puts it, "The worth of a librarian, I would gauge by his power of attracting and looking after ... circles (of readers), of acting as the intermediary for an intimacy of relationship between reader and library. That is to say, on him is cast the burden not only of the books, but of their readers as well. And in the maintenance of both is the test of his efficiency, of the proper discharge of his trust." (Tagore, 1929).

As the chief librarian his objective, therefore, is not to wield power for its own sake but to use it, as Tagore has pointed out, for popularising the library, increasing the membership, facilitating recreational, informational and investigative reading. In the context of today, equally important is the extension services that he has to carry out with the aim of eradicating illiteracy and helping the underprivileged educate themselves, conscientising them in the process so that they realise their inherent strength. This empowerment of the underprivileged will set in motion a series of changes that will improve their lot. The chief librarian could, thus, be gratified that the cultural movement that he and his team initiated was instrumental in paving the way for the betterment of the marginalised and the society in general.

Footnotes

1 This may comprise the HoDs, the Captain of the School, a representative each of the boys and girls of each class, the headmaster (chairman) and the librarian (secretary cum convenor).

2 It is better to refer to the staff as *co-workers* or *colleagues* than *subordinates*, the reason for which is explained a little later.

Appendix 1
A Few Selected Internet Sites

Search Engines

www.lii.org (Librarians' guide to the Internet)
www.altavista.digital.com (General)
www.aj.com (General – Jeeves Answers Adults)
www.ajkids.com (General – Children's 'Jeeves')
www.dogpile.com (Metasearch Engine)
www.excite.com (Excite)
www.google.com (Google)
www.googleguide.com (Get the best out of Google)
www.teoma.co.uk (Google favourite – General)
www.homeworkheaven.com (Homework)
www.hotbot.com (HotBot)
www.infind.com (Inference)
www.infoseek.com (InfoSeek)
www.isleuth.com (I Sleuth)
www.looksmart.com (Look Smart)
www.northernlight.com (Northernlight)
www.startingpoint.com (Starting Point)
www.lycos.com (Lycos)
www.mckinley.com (Magellan)
www.metacrawler.com (Metacrawler)
www.netscape.com (Netscape)

www.saveysearch.com (Saveysearch)
www.snap.com (Snap)
www.opentext.com (Opentext)
www.webcrawler.com (WebCrawler)
www.yahoo.com (Yahoo! Very popular)
www.searchenginewatch.com (A guide to searching)
www.searchengineshowdown.com (Less comprehensive)
www.ask.co.uk (Ask Jeeves any question – He answers)
www.mamma.com (The 'Mother of all Search Engines')
http://turbo10.com (Where major search engines don't go)
www.37.com ('Thirty-seven-in-One' search engine)
www.ungoogle.com (Useful when Google fails)
www.clusteredhits.com (US oriented)
www.scirus.com (Scientific information only)

Booksellers

www.bestbookbuys.com (Best prices – American)
www.amazon.co.uk (Books/Video/DVD/Games, etc.)
http://bookshop.blackwell.co.uk (Academic/Professional)
www.studentbook world.com (Academic books)
www.books.co.uk (For online booksellers)
www.swotbooks.co.uk (For low cost books)
www.greenmetropolis.com (Good condition second hand books)
www.bn.com (Barnes and Noble's site – Biggest bookseller)
www.bookpeople.co.uk (Discounted – children's & fiction)
www.compman.co.uk (Computer manuals)
www.crimetime.co.uk (Crime fiction)
www.bookbrain.co.uk (for competitive prices)
www.book-shops.net (for specialised bookstores-UK)

www.booktracker.co.uk (for competitive prices –UK)

Free Books on the Internet (For downloading)

http://www.booksbtc.com/free-books.htm

http://www.digital.library.upenn.edn/books/

http://www.ipl.org/reading/books/

http://classics.mit.edu

http://onlinebooks.library.upenn.edu

www.questia.com

History

www.oceanindex.net (35,000 links to external sites)

www.historyworld.net (History - World)

www.fordham.edu/halsall/india/indiasbook.html (Indian)

www.asterius.com/china (Chinese history - elementary)

http://sun.sino.uni-heidelberg.de/igcs (More links on China)

www.ancientgreece.com (On Ancient Greece)

http://web.uccs.edu/-history/index/japan.html (Japanese)

http://www.asianinfo.org/asianinfo/korea/history.html (Korean history)

www.friesian.com/turkia.htm (Ottoman Empire)

www.prc.org.uk/palestine%2048/history.html (Palestinian history)

www.hun.huji.ac.il/dinur/ (Biblical with 6000 links)

www.al.bab.com/arab/history.htm (Arab history)

www.the-orb.net (Mediaeval European history)

www.tau.ac.il/Germanhistory/links.html (Links to German history)

www.ukans.edu/history/VL (By country/historical periods)

www.academicinfo.net/histaus.html (Australian history)

www.roman-empire.net (Roman Empire)

http://chnm.gmu.edu/revolution (French Revolution)

www.sispain.org/rnglidh/history (Spanish with links)

www.users.dircon.co.uk (Spanish Civil War)

www.barnsdle.demon.co.uk/russ/rusrev.html (Russian Revolution – Glimpses)

www.departments.bucknell.edu/russian/history.html (Russian history – Comprehensive)

http://earlyamerica.com (Early history of America)

www.ancientmexico.com (Ancient Mexico/Aztec & Mayan Empires)

http://isers.snowcrest.net/jmike/latin.html (South/Latin America with links)

www.spartacus.schoolnet.com (History Encyclopaedia)

www.thehistorychannel.com (The best search in history)

Science

www.howstuffworks.com (Wide ranging)

www.voltnet.com (On Electricity)

www.world-mysteries.com (Mysteries of Science)

www.si.edu/science_and_technology (All branches of science)

www.funsci.com (Experiments – Simple and hard))

www.tryscience.org (Science/simple experiments for children)

www.doscience.com (Experiments – for children)

Nature & Environment

www.wildlifesearch.com (Links to sites on all animals)

www.umich.edu/~esupdate/ (Endangered species)

www.naturecom.de/eng/index.html (For Children)

http://netvet.wustl.edu/e-zoo.htm (Good for research)

www.animalworlddirectory.com (Articles on nature)

www.arkive.org (Awareness of endangered species)

Home

www.learn2.com (Helpful House Hints)

www.todayshomeowner.com (Helpful House Hints)

www.how2do.com (How to do anything)

www.incrediblyuseful.com (Useful Site of the Day)

Periodicals

www.childrrensbooktrust.co (Children's World - India)

www.thehindu.com (The Hindu - India)

www.thehindu.in (The Hindu - India)

www.theindpress.com (The New Indian Express)

www.historytoday.com (History magazine – World)

www.popsci.com (Popular Science)

www.sciencemag.org (Articles comprehensible to layman with links)

www.newscientist.com (New Scientist)

Dictionaries

www.oed.com(Oxford English Dictionary – on subscription)

www.cup.cam.ac.uk/elf/dictionary (Cambridge Dictionary

English & American English/Idioms

www.onelook.com (Access over 900 dictionaries)

www.wordorigins.org (Etymology of nearly 500 words and phrases)

www.thesaurus.com (Based on Roget's Thesaurus)

http://phrases.shu.ac.uk (Over 2000 phrases & sayings explained)

www.acronymfinder.com (More than a lakh and a half acronyms)

www.peevish.co.uk/slang (Slangs – UK)

www.netdictionary.com (Internet terms)

Encyclopaedias

www.eb.com (Britannica – on payment)

http://encarta.msn.com (Encarta encyclopaedia)

www.encyclopaedia.com (On-line encyclopaedia – Free)

www.infoplease.com (Almanacs/Encyclopaedia/Atlas)

www.utm.edu/research/iep (Internet encyclopaedia of philosophy)

http://plato.stansford.edu (Stansford Encyclopaedia of philosophy)

www.babloo.com (Encyclopaedia for children)

Publishers (Indian)

www.childrrensbooktrust.co (Children's books)

www.essessreference.com (Books on Library Science)

www.leftword.com (Left oriented books)

E-books

www.free-ebooks.net (Free e-books)

www.netlibrary.com (Wide choice)

www.bartleby.com/ebook (Classics/other free e-books)

www.fictionwise.com (Fiction/Non-fiction – wide choice)

Second hand books

www.abebooks.com (Access to 50 million used, rare books)

www.booklovers.co.uk (Quality second hand books)

www.bibliofind.com (A search engine from Amazon)

www.bookfinder.com (A wider search engine)

www.hp.bookfinders.co.uk (A UK based service)

www.shapero.com (Natural history and travel-related books)

Children's Books (Useful for Book Selection

www.achuka.co.uk (Reviews, Author interviews)

www.carolhurst.com (Great for book reviews)

www.centreforthechildrensbook.org.uk (Opening 2005)

www.childrensbookshop.com (Traditional site)

www.wordpool.co.uk (For advice on what to read)

www.usbourne.com (Specialist publisher)

www.ukchildrensbooks.co.uk (List of links to Sites)

www.ulcalgary.ca/-dkbrown/ (Excellent children's literature)

www.wordsofdiscovery.com (Books with positive view of life)

www.worldbookday.com (About World Book Day)

General

www.guinnessrecords.com (World Records)

www.mythweb.com (Greek myths – illustrated)

Appendix 2
A Brief History of the Catalogue

Had it not been for the discovery of printing and the proliferation of printed books the trading class called booksellers would not have arisen. It may not be wrong to say that the birthplace of this trade was Germany, chiefly at Frankfurt on the Maine, where booksellers from all around come and set up shop especially at the time of the fairs. And it was the business compulsions of this class of traders who specialised in the sale of books that brought forth what is known as the 'catalogue', which was a list of books brought out by a printer and its only objective was promotion of the sale of those books.

The credit for conceiving the idea of such a catalogue goes to George Willer, an enterprising businessman of Augsburg in Germany who had a large bookshop. He was a familiar figure at the fairs and he printed a catalogue of all the new books, giving their titles and sizes. Le Mire, a clergyman, in his book mentions that this catalogue appeared in the year 1554. Willer's catalogues continued to be printed for thirty-eight years, till 1592 by Nicol Bassaeus, a printer of Frankfort and after Willer's death it was published by Henning Grosse, a Leipzig book seller, and by his son and grandson. This paved the way for several such catalogues but no other surpassed that of Willer's. Since Willer's death, however, the booksellers had been constrained to migrate to Leipzig because of the various restrictions on the printing of catalogues imposed by the Council of Frankfurt.

All the catalogues that the printers brought out following in Willer's footsteps, were in quarto and not paginated In Willer's catalogues, books were classified, with Latin books topping the list and of these, priority was given to Protestant theological works, maybe because Wilier was a Lutheran. This was followed by works of Catholic theology, after which were printed books of jurisprudence, medicine, philosophy, poetry and music. After all these, were listed books published in the German language, subject-wise, in the same order.

Two catalogues worth mentioning are collections of all the catalogues published at different fairs in different years, brought out at the request of some booksellers. The first, which appeared in the late 16th century was published by Joanne Clessio, under the formidable title, *Unius saeculi ejusque virorum litteratorum monumentis tum florentissimi, tum fertilissimi, ab anno 1500 ad 1602 nundinarum autmnalium inclusive, elenchus consummatissimus — desumutus partim ex singularum nundinarum catalogis, partim ex bibliothecis. Auctore, Joanne Clessio, Wineccensi, Hannoio, philosopho ac medic.* Another remarkable catalogue was that of Draudius. It was in several quarto volumes and was printed first in 1611 and later in an enlarged edition, which was more comprehensive and systematic, in 1625. One part, believed to be the first, of this work contains Latin works on theology, jurisprudence, medicine, history, geography and politics. In the copy extant and held by the library of the University of Gottingen, the first part ends at page 1304, with a catchword indicating a deficiency. And the second part, which also contains Latin books, begins at page 1298 (?) and ends with page 1654, followed by an Index of the authors mentioned therein. Another smaller volume of 302 pages has no index and there is also a fourth part containing 759 pages excluding an index of the authors, which is a catalogue of all the books printed in the German language till 1625.It was only in 1595 that the first ever catalogue of English books on sale saw the light of day. Consisting of two parts, this was brought out in folio by Andrew Maunsell, a London bookseller, in folio in two parts, with the first part containing the names of books on *Divinity* and the second, listing books of *Arts* and *Sciences.* It is said, he had planned to publish a third part containing *History* and *Political Literature* but, for some reason or other, it did not materialise.

The booksellers of Leipzig, which was known for its traditional book publishing industry and annual fairs, brought out a general Easter Catalogue in 1604, with the permission of the Government. And after that the Leipzig booksellers began to reprint the Frankfurt catalogues, with many additional entries of books that were not brought to Frankfurt. Later, Georg, another printer, collected all the previously published catalogues and brought out a catalogue titled *Bucher Lexicon* which was a catalogue printed in Europe, brought up to 1750; with supplements to 1758, 8 parts in 4 volumes folio. This was an elaborate compilation, which includes all the books known at that time and even those printed in 1462, giving the title, place of publication, name of publisher, date, size, number of leaves and published price of all of them. By the end of the 17th century and during the 18th century most booksellers began to bring out catalogues of all types in large numbers, the most remarkable of which being Henry Bonn's *Guinea Catalogue,* a detailed publication of his own stock, which was over 15 cm thick, with about 2000 pages.

The drawback with most of those catalogues is that they have included many books, which have not been printed and many titles, names and dates have been given wrongly. Nevertheless, these do help a scholar researching the history of literature.[1]

---

1 This brief history is based on an article included in *A History of Inventions and Discoveries, and Origins* by John Beckmann.

References

Barnett, A., Libraries, Community and Technology, McFarland & Co., Jefferson, 2002.

Beckman, J., A History of Inventions and Discoveries, and Origins, V.2., *Tr.* by W. Johnston, Henry G. Bohn, London, 1846.

Blanchard, K., *et al.*, Leadership and the One Minute Manager, William Morrow and Co., New York, 1985.

Chander Prakash, Computers in Library and Information science, Zee Publications, New Delhi, 2000.

Cornforth, M., Dialectical Materialism, Calcutta, 1976.

Cutter, C.A., Rules for a Dictionary Catalogue, Washington, 1904.

Dange, S.A., India, Bombay, 1951.

Dewey, M., Decimal Classification and Relative Index, V.1, Forest Press, New York, 1951.

Dutta, D., An Introduction to Library Cataloguing, The World Press, Calcutta, 1958.

Engels, F., Dialectics of Nature, Progress Publishers, Moscow, 1974.

Evans, G., Management Techniques for Libraries, Academic Press, New York, 1983.

Freire, P., Cultural Action for Freedom, Penguin Books, Hammondsworth, 1977.

Goswami, I.M., Manual of Library Cataloguing, Commonwealth Publishers, New Delhi, 1995.

Gray, D., Fundamentals of Librarianship, George Allen and Unwin, London, 1949.

Hawkins, E., Expansive Classification. In *Encyclopaedia of Librarianship*, ed. by T. Landau, Bowes and Bowes, London, 1961.

Hindu, The, The Hindu Speaks on Management, 2V., Kasturi & Sons, Chennai, 2003.

Howard, P.W., A Primer of Book Classification, A.A.L., London, 1955.

Indian Council of Agricultural Research, The Indian Agricultural Sciences Abstracts, New Delhi, 2003.

Krishan Kumar, Library Administration and Management, Vikas, New Delhi, 1987.

Krishan Kumar, Reference Service, Vikas, New Delhi, 1984.

Krishnamurthy, R., Library management, Commonwealth Publishers, N. Delhi, 1997.

Lakshmanaswami Mudaliar, A., Report of the Secondary Education Commission, 1953.

Lenin, V.I., The Tasks of Public Library in Petrograd. In *Lenin and Library Organisation*, Comp. by K. I. Abramov, Moscow, 1977.

Leyland, E., Libraries in Schools, Oldbourne, London, 1961.

Lloyd, G.A., Universal Decimal Classification. In *Encyclopaedia of Librarianship*, ed. by T. Landau, Bowes and Bowes, London, 1961.

Lloyd, H., Physical and Reference Bibliography. In *The library*, V. 20, 1965.

McColvin, L, How to Find Out, Rochester, 1933.

McColvin, L.R., Libraries for Children, Phoenix, London, 1961.

Macdonnel, A.A., A History of Sanskrit Literature, Varanasi, 1971.

Mohanraj, V.M., Library Services for Children, Ess Ess Publications, New Delhi, 2004.

Morgan, L.H., Ancient Society, Henry Holt & Co., New York, 1978.

Mulla, K.R., Library and Internet: via Cable Network – A Propose. In *SRELS Journal of Information Management*, V.41, No.2.

Radhakrishnan, S., The Library Movement. In *The Library Movement*, A collection of essays, by Diverse Hands, MLA, Madras, 1929.

Ralph, R.G., The Library in Education, Phoenix House, London, 1960.

Ranganathan, S.R., Classified Catalogue Code, Asia, Bombay, 1964.

Ranganathan, S.R., Five Laws of Library Science, University of Delhi, New Delhi, 1951.

Ranganathan, S.R., Library Development Plan, University of Delhi, Delhi, 1950.

Sharma, N.K., Management Technique, Jaipur, 1995.

Swihart, S.J. and Hefley, B.F., Computer Systems in the Library, Melville Publishing Co., Los Angeles, 1973.

Tagore, R., What Makes a Library Good. In *The Library Movement* by Diverse Hands, MLA, Madras, 1929.

Wallace, A.R., Contributions to the Theory of Natural Selection, London, 1870.

World Book Dictionary, V.2, Chicago, 1981.

Young, H., et al, *Eds.*, Glossary of Library and Information Science, ALA, Chicago, 1983.

Index